£4.95

Recollections of
SALFORD

Articles written by members and friends of the Salford Local History Society

Edited by
Ted Gray & Cliff Hayes

PRINTWISE PUBLICATIONS LIMITED
1992

© Printwise Publications Limited
1992

05583425

Published by Printwise Publications Limited
47 Bradshaw Road,
Tottington,
Bury,
Lancs,
BL8 3PW.

Warehouse and Orders
40–42 Willan Industrial Estate,
Vere Street (off Eccles New Road),
Salford, M5 2GR.
Tel: 061–745 9168
Fax: 061–737 1755

ISBN 1 872226 63 9

Book idea by

Cliff Hayes

Printed and bound by Manchester Free Press,
Paragon Mill, Jersey Street, Manchester M4 6FP
Tel: 061–236 8822

Cover pictures: How many features did you spot? They include an identity card, Clothing Coupon book, and coupons for Utility Furniture (all from the 1939-45 War), plus a photograph of Pilot Officer Douglas Ackerley, of Patricroft, who was killed when his aircraft was shot down over Holland; a tram ticket and a picture of a route 70 tram; railway tickets from Salford and Seedley stations; a brass twopenny token; postcards of the Docks, Ordsall Hall, Cross Lane junction and Pendleton Church; a postcard from a sailor in Salford Docks telling his family of his forthcoming voyage; a programme from the Regent Theatre; a 1915 license for a tramcar conductoress; a notice from the 'talking pictures' at the Seedley Cinema; a letter-head from the Ordsall Lane firm of Sir W.H. Bailey; and family snapshots. The rear cover is not quite the same as the front — can you spot the differences?

FOREWORD

By The Chairman of Salford Local History Society

The poet Thomas Hood claimed to remember the house where he was born,
>"The little window where the sun
>Came peeping in at morn."

Another writer, Thomas Moore, in 1815 described how,
>"Oft in the stilly night.
>Ere slumber's chain has bound me,
>Fond memory brings the light
>Of other days around me."

The pages which follow indicate how many Salford people do remember, not necessarily where they were born, but the incidents which coloured their early years and the characters who populated their environment and helped form their lives. This book is the culmination of a project aimed at setting down the recollections of some of the 200 members of the Salford Local History Society. The City Of Salford has changed radically over the past thirty years: It has altered in area, because of local government boundary changes ; in size of population because of demographic fluctuations ; and in its industrial, social, and recreational make-up. Society members believe that it is important for future generations to have a glimpse of what life was like before the age of lap-top computers, microwave ovens, and instant world-wide communications. This book does not attempt to cover all aspects of life, but it is hoped that the various articles will give a taste of Salford as it was, which readers will enjoy and which may cause them to reflect on their own times past.

As Chairman, I am pleased that so many people have been able to contribute, and that the Society has such a helpful friends at Printwise Publications to publish our work. Over the years individual members have produced books and cards, have helped with cataloguing at the Local History Library in Peel Park, and have mounted exhibitions for the now-defunct Salford Show. Indeed, the Society was proud to be the winner of the first-ever award for 'Best Exhibition' at the Show. In the words of our first Newsletter, "we are a friendly society," and we aim to continue to encourage the study of local history in all its aspects.

I hope that 'Recollections Of Salford,' the Society's first joint publication, will both maintain our aim and provide a knowledgeable and nostalgic look-back at people and events in the history of our proud city.

Don Rainger

ACKNOWLEDGEMENTS

The Salford Local History Society is indebted to a number of people who have made possible the production of this book. The idea of compiling an anthology of short articles and reminiscences came from Cliff Hayes, of Printwise Publications, Salford, who first suggested that members should be invited to record their memories, or to write pieces on their own particular interests. Cliff has exercised a guiding hand during the period of preparation, and has seen the project through to publication. Cliff is an enthusiastic and energetic publisher of books of local interest, and 'Recollections Of Salford' is another title to add to his list. We appreciate his support and guidance. We are indebted to those who have allowed pictures to be reproduced, including Harold Riley, M. J. O'Connor, the 'Salford Journal,' and 'The Guardian.' Thanks are due to D. Rendell Photographic Services, of Hale, for preparation of prints etc.

The staff of the Salford Local History Library (Tim Ashworth, Tony Frankland, Sandra Hayton, and Patricia Nuttall) have been of tremendous help in seeking out suitable illustrations, finding the answers to assorted queries, and offering general guidance.

After an initial period of doubt, during which it was wondered whether enough material would be submitted, contributions came in from nearly fifty members and friends of the Society. The articles cover a wide range of topics, and we hope that there will be something to appeal to all tastes. We thank all those who took the trouble to set down their ideas on paper, and we hope they will be pleased with the result.

Salford Local History Society

If you are interested in Local History, why not join the Salford Local History Society? Meetings are held on the last Tuesday of every month (except December), commencing at 7.30 pm, in Midwood Hall, 1, Eccles Old Road, Pendleton, Salford, M6 7AE. The Society is a friendly group of people, formed to encourage and facilitate the study of all aspects of Salford's past. Meetings take the form of slide shows, lectures, or discussions, and are not too intellectual or academic, so do not be put off. The topics included in this book form a representative sample of the sort of themes chosen for our meetings. In addition, a monthly newsletter is issued to members, and visits to places of interest are arranged in the summer months. Why not come along as a guest to one of our meetings? Midwood Hall is situated close to the junction of Eccles Old Road and Bolton Road, and buses stop nearby.

'RECOLLECTIONS OF SALFORD'

Contents

Contents — *continued*

Agecroft Rowing Club

George Crompton

There is very little left of the old Whit Lane now because most of it was demolished under the Council's clearance programme and replaced by a modern housing estate. The 'Old House At Home' is still there (what a lovely name for a pub), but the nearby butcher's shop where I was born 73 years ago has gone.

The street at the side of our shop was named Irwell Street because at one time it ran directly from Whit Lane to the banks of the river. Later on, a high wall, incorporating two large gates, was built across the bottom of the street to enclose the boathouse of the Agecroft Rowing Club.

When I was a small boy, we used to play games on the cinder croft in front of the gates. Our games would be interrupted by the arrival of the oarsmen, when the gates would be opened to admit them to the Club, and for a moment we would be able to see the swift-flowing waters of the Irwell.

Any account of life in Whit Lane would be incomplete without explaining how the Agecroft Rowing Club came to be situated in such a heavily-populated area. The early history of the Club is recorded in Log Books, now deposited in the archives of the John Rylands Library in Manchester, from where I obtained much of this information.

The founder of the Club was Ishmael Lythgoe, a Manchester businessman who, in 1860, along with his friend Mr. Thorpe, decided to keep a boat on the River Irwell at Agecroft. His recorded purpose was "for the pleasure of an occasional row in our leisure hours, and because physical development and healthy recreation are absolutely necessary for those who work in the surroundings of City life. Rowing has long held a very high position in the list of manly exercises, and, doubtless, has been an essential element in the education of the bravest and ablest defenders of our Country - for no pastime can equal rowing for strengthening the limbs, or drawing out those cordial social qualities of the heart which are inevitably the results of pulling together."

Lythgoe and Thorpe were unsuccessful in attempts to gain permission to erect a landing stage near Drinkwater Park, but the owner of the Kersal Vale Printing Works offered them the use of an old boiler house near the river bank. There, they built a wooden landing stage and bought their first boat for £3·00.

In June 1864 a meeting was held at the Kersal Hotel, in Moor Lane, Salford, where it was agreed that those who were accepted as members of the new Club should pay an annual subscription of ten shillings per year, plus one shilling per month. It was decided to invite tenders for the construction of a new boathouse on the Pendleton side of the river. This became an urgent necessity when the original landing stage was swept away during the Great Flood of 1866, but sufficient progress was made to enable the first official 'Opening Day of the Rowing Season' to be held in the same year. So it was that the Agecroft Rowing Club came to be established on the Whit Lane, Pendleton, bank of the Irwell, where it remained until 1935.

In spite of the heavily-polluted river and the background of grimy and smoky factory chimneys, the Club continued to attract new members, including oarsmen of the calibre of Dr.S.M.Boyd, who became the Amateur Rowing Champion of Ireland, and John B. Close Brooke, a Cambridge Blue, who won the Diamond Sculls at Henley in 1870.

An episode in 1874 illustrates the class divisions of the early years. The Bolton & Ringley Rowing Club entered a crew in a four-oared race for a silver plate and a prize of £10. Bolton & Ringley won, but were afterwards disqualified because they had not disclosed that members of their crew were 'working men.' The action of the Agecroft committee aroused strong feelings. A letter was published in a Manchester newspaper which said that the disqualification of the winning crew because it was composed of colliers, and not 'gentlemen,' showed a "spirit of snobbish injustice and narrowness of views quite incompatible with the principles of *real* gentlemen." The Club secretary responded, "The advertisement for the race stated that it would

Agecroft Regatta in the 1950s. The post-war club house may be seen on the far bank of the River Irwell, with the buildings of Kersal Cell in the background.

be rowed in boats provided by the committee, by *gentlemen* who had never won a four-oared race at a regatta. As the race progressed, it was evident that the men from the Bolton & Ringley Club were sturdy working men of the class known as artisans. They row, or rather pull, with such power and persistence that, despite the utmost efforts of gentlemen who make the art of rowing a study for their leisure hours, they are defeated by these men by sheer brute force. We took a broad view of the question, and it is not unlikely that these men (very decent in their way) might have misread the disqualification or may not have been able to read it."

This disparaging reference was answered by the Secretary of the Bolton & Ringley Club, who wrote that his members, strictly amateurs, could not have accepted the prize money, as the Club rules did not allow it, but they would have liked to hold the trophy. He added, "Our entry was a result of the friendship between the oarsmen of the two clubs. Is not a working man who is honest in all his dealings as much a gentleman as one with a good coat on? It is not money which makes a gentleman, but good deeds. I hope that the Agecroft Rowing Club will reconsider their decision and give the trophy to the crew who fairly won it."

There is no record of the decision being reversed, but the affair caught the attention of the national press and the argument raged on for some months. A supporter of the disqualification wrote sarcastically, "We have all heard about working men drinking champagne and travelling first class, and this probable further attempt at social elevation influenced the decision of the Committee." Another pointed out that a successful artisan, who might be a wealthy man and a large employer of labour, could be debarred, whilst a clerk in his employ would be able to apply for membership.

The Club weathered the storm, and entries to their annual regatta continued to grow in number.

Even as late as 1932, there were 60 entries, from rowing clubs in all parts of the kingdom, including colleges in Oxford and Cambridge. Local competitors included the Broughton Rowing Club and the Manchester University Boat Club.

The increasing pollution of the river was a severe problem for those who had to row on it. One member described it thus:

This is as a river as black as ink,
That flows thickly by, and kicks up a stink,
And fills your nostrils and makes you blink

By the turn of the century, the scene upon which the original members of the Agecroft Rowing Club had gazed, had undergone a marked change. One press report read: "The ancient riverside footpath remains, but smoke-begrimed buildings crowd upon it, and a once-picturesque portion of the valley is no longer to be seen. What the river itself has become, there is no need to say, suffice that members of the Agecroft Rowing Club continue to patronise it as though it was still a river and not a sewer, and are every bit as enthusiastic in pursuit of their sport as their more favoured brethren who live on the banks of the Thames, the Mersey, the Dee, or the Trent. *Nothing but the absolute solidification of the mixture occupying the course of the Irwell will drive them off.*"

There was always a carnival atmosphere in Whit Lane on Regatta Day, almost as though the Whit Laners felt that they had some part to play in the festivities. Streets were decorated with bunting, and a fair was held on the river bank. All day long, cars, taxis, and boat-transporters pulled up to the Clubhouse, or on to Lewis's field, where a marquee was erected to serve refreshments to members, guests, and local dignitaries. Girls in pretty frocks and young men wearing Club caps and blazers added colour to the scene, and the Pendleton Public Prize Band played throughout the day.

The field adjoining the Clubhouse belonged to George Lewis, and remembering how 'Cocky' Lewis, who kept pigs and poultry, had regularly chased children from his property, I was interested to read the Secretary's warning to Regatta organisers: "Mr.Lewis is a well-lined man, and responds gladly to friendliness, but he will not be high-hatted on any account, and so long as we are dependent upon his good offices, hot-blooded Captains and imperious secretaries will be well-advised to bear this in mind."

These remarks might well have been applied to most Whit Lane folk, who, whilst enjoying the 'goings-on,' considered themselves just as good, although not as fortunate, as the invited guests and paying spectators who were admitted to Lewis's field. The majority of Whit Laners lined the banks of the river further down the course, always cheering the Agecroft crew, and occasionally enjoying the spectacle of an upturned boat.

My father rented a piece of derelict land from "Sammy Ashton's Dyeworks" next to the Club,

The former Club House of the Agecroft Rowing Club at Giant's Seat, Ringley.

and this wasteland was transformed by my grandfather, a retired joiner, into a pleasant backwater, with a putting green, summer house, and a small riverside walk. This meant that we were lucky enough to have a grandstand view of the boat races. On one occasion, a skiff overturned, and the sole occupant, a big man with a red face, attempted to return to the starting line by swimming, pushing the upturned boat in front of him. Whether it was the stench, the slime, or the rats (which could often be seen swimming near the surface), I do not know, but he changed his mind, and came ashore where I was standing with some of my friends. "Which is the quickest way back to the Agecroft Rowing Club?" he asked in a choking voice. I told him that there was no short cut, and that he would have to walk back along Whit Lane. I shall never forget the sight of this big man, in his baggy shorts and ankle socks, dripping with evil-smelling mud, marching solemnly down Whit Lane carrying the inverted boat on top of his head. This provided much amusement for the passers-by, and the crowd of children who followed him back to the boathouse.

There is a river filled with mud,
'Tis drawn from Salford's drains,
And oarsmen plunged beneath the flood,
Come out with filthy stains.

At the end of Regatta Day, the pubs were full of rowers celebrating or commiserating. Waiting outside, would be groups of children. When the 'toffs' emerged, the children would cry "Scabs, mister?" and, more often than not, a handful of loose change would be showered over their heads, resulting in an enjoyable scramble. Pandemonium would reign for a few minutes.

Members of the Agecroft Club were allowed to row on the Manchester, Bury and Bolton Canal, which adjoins the river for much of its length. On sunny days during the season, this was a route of escape to Ringley, an old village in a pleasant, wooded part of the Irwell valley. The Club rented a large house, called Giant's Seat, which had previously been the home of the Canal Manager. This house was large enough to boast a small ballroom, so dances and social evenings were held there. Sadly, today it would be impossible to use the canal, which is no longer navigable.

In 1935, the year of King George V's Silver Jubilee, the Salford Council decided that the extensive playing fields on the Kersal side of the river should be made more easily accessible for the residents of Pendleton. A footbridge over the river was therefore constructed at the bottom end of Irwell Street. It was named 'Jubilee Bridge.'

The old Clubhouse came to be rented by Manchester University, until it was irreparably damaged by German bombs which fell on the adjacent dye works during the 'Christmas Blitz' in 1940. The Agecroft Rowing Club was re-located, returning to the other side of the river near Kersal Cell, not very far from the spot where Lythgoe and Thorpe had sought permission to erect a landing stage some 75 years earlier.

Despite many problems, in July 1945 the Agecroft Rowing Club held its first Regatta on the Irwell since 1939. The event was re-established, and the crowds returned to the banks of the river on the big day. The spectators, however, were very different from those described by a writer of 1904, "On the Kersal side, fashion foregathers, gloriously apparelled, whilst on the Pendleton side, raggedness airs itself." Many of today's spectators are families who arrive in their own cars for a day out by the river, watching a sport of which they know but little, but still hoping (I suspect) to see an upturned boat or two, just as I did 60 years ago.

In 1958 Salford City Council, with assistance from the Government's Inner Cities Aid Programme, took over the Club's premises and facilities for a nominal sum, whilst allowing the Agecroft Rowing Club and the Salford University Rowing Club to remain as tenants. The reconstruction and modernisation of the boathouse has benefitted many local children, who will now be able to use the Club's twenty racing boats, and take advantage of the experience of the oarsmen. The future now looks bright for Salford's last surviving rowing club, which has the promise of new premises in the Salford Quays redevelopment scheme, where, it is hoped, a regional and national rowing centre will be established.

In 1932 the Club Secretary wrote, "There is a waning interest in rowing, because of the growing popularity of other sports." How surprised he would have been in 1984 to read in 'The Guardian' that "rowing on the Irwell has become the fastest-growing sport in Salford, and it is possible that the North will produce more oarsmen than footballers."

Broughton Road area in the 1920s & 1930s

Eric Brogan

The former 'Bijou' Cinema on Broughton Road is well-remembered by those who grew up in the neighbourhood. On Saturday afternoons, the children's matinee was a joyous occasion. To sit on a wooden bench cost only a penny, but to relax in luxury in the back two rows of separate upholstered seats cost twopence. Mr. Jones, a large man who (so childish gossip said) had a wooden leg, collected the money, but no tickets were issued. I used to go with twopence, one for admission, the other for two half-penny 'nuggets' (bars of Roocroft's nougat). A great cheer went up when the pianist walked down the aisle to start the show. The pianist was a Mr. Salisbury, who lived a few doors from the 'Bijou' and taught the piano.

Emlyn Jenkins, the Salford Rugby Club half-back, was made Assistant Manager at the Ambassador Cinema in Langworthy Road, and, possibly in retaliation, Gus Risman was then appointed as Assistant Manager at the Scala in Ford Lane. As children, we used to go along just to stand outside hoping to catch a glimpse of our heroes, both of them Welsh international players. But in their respective foyers, both seemed different in the unfamiliar garb of evening dress.

The old L.M.S. Railway used to run Saturday evening trips to Blackpool, and we could catch the train at Pendleton New (Broad Street) Station at about 6.30pm, returning at 11.30pm. The excursion return ticket cost two shillings for adults, but an additional sixpence would secure admission to the Tower or the Winter Gardens. As a 13-year-old, I travelled for half fare, just one shilling. When there was a race meeting scheduled at Castle Irwell, trains consisting entirely of horse-boxes would pull in at Pendleton Old Station, and the horses would be led off over the platform into Brettargh Street, then formed into single file to be walked down Broughton Road and Cromwell Road to the Racecourse. This station was sometimes used for sheep and cattle destined for the Cross Lane Cattle Market. On these occasions, the animals would be herded along Cheltenham Street and Frederick Road.

Halton Bank School on Bolton Road was built in 1908. Now no longer used as a school, the building is currently being converted into a hotel and apartments.

On the first occasion when the Albion Racecourse presented Speedway Racing, the management advertised a concession - ladies would be admitted free of charge. That evening I was standing outside watching people enter, when someone pulled me into the middle of a crowd of ladies, and in a few moments I was inside the stadium. The speedway stars I remember well include Eric Langton, Frank Varey, Oliver Langton, 'Squib' Burton, and 'Sprouts' Elder. The Castle Irwell Racecourse across the way was the assembly point for those taking part in the annual procession in aid of Salford Royal Hospital. Judging and the presentation of awards in the various categories (horse-drawn vehicles, brass bands, fancy dress, decorated floats, etc.) took place before the start, and then the long column would leave via Cromwell Road, Whit Lane, and Broad Street to reach the hospital on The Crescent. Money was collected en route, rather like the students' Shrove Tuesday Rag event.

A length of the Manchester, Bury and Bolton canal lay alongside the railway near Broughton Road, and here boys used to swim without costumes, trunks, or towels. Some daring individuals would dive to the bottom to pick up lumps of coal which had fallen from the barges.

There was a toy shop in Whit Lane run by Sammy Hoffman. It became generally known that on New Year's Day he was worth a visit. Children came from miles around, went into the shop and wished Sammy a cheery "Happy New Year." Sammy always produced a small gift for each one.

On Saturday evenings both the 'Manchester Evening News' and the 'Manchester Evening Chronicle' issued special football editions containing all the results. The papers were brought by motor van to

Before the Second World War, all Salford parks had lakes. Here is the one in Seedley Park, where the writer fed the ducks.

Broad Street, near St. Thomas's Church, where they were handed over to young men on bicycles. The cycles were stripped of all unnecessary items, such as mud-guards, to keep them as lightweight as possible. A race would develop between the 'News Boys' and the 'Chron Boys,' all downhill along Broughton Road, to see who could arrive first, and presumably sell most papers, in Whit Lane and Langley Road.

I attended Halton Bank School, from where we walked to Seedley Baths for our swimming lessons. On the return journey it became a ritual for some of us to buy a bag of broken biscuits for a half-penny. We ate most of them, but also fed the ducks on Seedley Park pond. Wall's ice cream, purchased from the 'Stop Me And Buy One' tricycles with the large ice-box in front, were favourites if you could afford them - a 'Snofruit' for a penny, brick-ette for twopence. Some of the men would cut a 'Snofruit' into two pieces, and sell each for a half-penny. At about 7.00pm each evening, the Wall's ice cream sellers would return to their depot, and we often saw them pushing their heavy tricycles uphill along Broughton Road and Broad Street. Sometimes an offer of assistance would be rewarded with half a 'Snofruit.'

At Christmas time a high spot of the season was the annual pantomime presented by members of the Salford City Police Force at the Palace Theatre in Cross Lane. There were no women in the Force, so all the parts were taken by men. The 'leading lady' (i.e. Cinderella, or whoever) was usually a hefty sergeant, and the chorus line seemed to consist of the stoutest constables. The singing was always good, and the shows, in aid of charities, were always well-supported.

My father smoked Wills' "Gold Flake" cigarettes, costing one shilling for a packet of 20, and in the days when small 'cigarette cards' were popular, there were always two in each pack. Several series were issued, and when 52 different cards had been collected, they could be mounted in an album, or sometimes exchanged for a full-size pack of playing cards. If you collected and 'swopped' with great determination, you could acquire even greater gifts, and in this way we gained a Bridge Set, consisting of two packs of cards in a leather case, complete with score cards, and eventually a beautiful folding card table with a green baize surface.

Childhood Memories

Pendleton — Joan Gaskell (née Heywood)

I was born in 1917, not long before the end of the Great War. My earliest memories must have been from when I was two or three years old, about the time when we moved to number 13 New Holland Street, Pendleton, a small two-up two-down terraced house with a back-yard, which had an outside lavatory. A feature of the back-yard was the big tin bath, which was always hanging on the wall by the scullery window.

The house had a walk-in door, opening directly from the street into the front room, a kitchen with a big black iron range, and a scullery, fitted with a small cast-iron fire-place and a bricked-in boiler. The boiler was filled with cold water on Mondays for the wash day chores, and on Fridays for bath-night in the tub. It was heated by a coal fire underneath. Next to it was the slop-stone, a shallow sink with only a cold-water tap and a tin bowl. The bowl had general uses, for washing pots, hands and faces, etc. Main features of the scullery were the items for use on the weekly wash-day - the 'dolly tub' and its 'posser,' (for churning the garments in the wash), and the large, wooden-rollered mangle, for squeezing water out of the washed clothes before hanging them out to dry.

A staircase led from the scullery to the two bedrooms, both of which had a small cast-iron grate, or fire-place. Fires were lit upstairs only when someone was ill.

I remember the milk-man coming round every day with his horse-and-cart, laden with milk churns, from which he ladled out gills, pints, or quarts with metal measures. Occasionally, a man with a sack over his shoulder came round, shouting "Messina Lemons."

Games were played outside in the street, and there seemed to be an unwritten, but regular pattern to the times of the year when certain activities recommenced. There was hopscotch, with squares chalked out on the paving stones ; skipping, using either a proper skipping rope with handles, or a long, scratchy piece of rope which we obtained free for the asking from the greengrocer, who I think had used it to tie up crates of fruit and vegetables ; and another game called 'Bobbers and Kibs,' which I cannot recall how to play.

I always enjoyed the yearly fair, which was held on the croft on Langworthy Road, opposite the school and next to the Friends' Meeting House, which had iron railings all round it.

I attended Langworthy Road School, and was taught there by a Miss Chorley, who had also taught my mother. Later, I gained a scholarship to the Salford Secondary School for Girls, near Bexley Square. About 1930 I was one of the many pupils who took part in the Salford Pageant in Buile Hill Park. Our history teacher, Miss Canning, was helping out with the historical details.

I came from a poor family, but those were happy days of childhood. Seedley Park and Buile Hill Park were ideal playgrounds, where we could play in perfect safety - though we had to behave ourselves, or the 'parky' would let us know in no uncertain manner!

Schooldays – *John Nugent*

As a child I attended St.Luke's C.of E.School in Salford, moving from the Infant Department to the Juniors when I was seven years old. One of my first lessons in the new school was at the Swimming Baths in Derby Road, Seedley. My class was marched to the baths, where the teacher, Mr.Davis, began to teach us 'dry land swimming' - that is to say, he taught us the movements of the breast stroke without entering the water. To give us an incentive, he held up a shilling and said, "This is for the first one to swim a length."

I immediately dived in, swam two lengths, climbed out and held my hand out for the 'bob.' What poor Mr. Davis did not know, was that for the past two or three years my mother had been giving me, and my older brothers, Billy and Peter, a half-penny every Saturday to go to the baths. This was our weekly bath, and my brothers had taught me to swim. But, nevertheless, I would have walked on water to earn that shilling!

My first poetry lesson was taken by the Headmaster, Mr. Quinn. He ensured that everybody had a poetry book, and, glancing at the big clock on the wall, he said, "It is twenty minutes past ten o'clock. I will be back in an hour, and I expect everyone to have memorised a poem by then."

Spotting that Mr. Quinn had mistaken the time, I called out, "It's twenty-five past, sir." Knowing that his pupils would choose a very short poem, he said to me, "All right, clever clogs, you can learn a longer poem than anyone else."

Flicking through the pages of the book, I came across 'Widdecombe Fair,' which, as everybody knows, appears to be a very long poem, but which has a much-repeated 'chorus' between the lines which tell the story. When the Headmaster returned he said, "Right, Nugent. Stand up on your chair, and recite your poem." As I began the first line, "Tom Pearce, Tom Pearce, lend me your grey

Langworthy Road School, opened in 1899, attended by Joan Gaskell, was used as a Military Hospital in the 1914-18 War.

Buile Hill Park where Joan Gaskell and her friends played under the watchful eye of the 'parky'.

mare," his face broke into a smile, and he made the rest of the class stand to give me a clap.

In the part of Salford where I lived was a small area of grassed land called the 'Sheep Field.' This was separated from the railway by metal railings, about six feet high aand surmounted by pointed tips. In company with my friends, I had torn and patched trousers which bore testimony to the sharpness of those pointed railings.

Our local 'bobby' was known as P.C.'Flycatcher.' He was a giant of a man, well over six feet tall, and appearing even taller when wearing his helmet. As he made his ponderous way around the neighbourhood, he always had his mouth open - hence his nickname. He was an old-fashioned policeman. I never saw him arrest anybody, but there was many a Saturday-night brawl outside the local pub that he broke up just by being there.

I am ashamed to admit that there were times when, with my pals, I trespassed on the railway. On one such occasion my friend and neighbour Harry Gresty, then aged seven, managed to get his foot stuck underneath the railway line. There were six or seven boys there, including me, and we knew that a train would be along shortly. We pushed and pulled at Harry to no effect, and began to shout and scream for help. We then saw the huge figure of P.C.'Flycatcher' galloping across the Sheep Field. It was not until his helmet fell off that I appreciated that policemen had hair.

With his great stride, he cleared the railings, and soon had hold of Harry's foot. "Grab hold of him, lads, and when I say so, pull." He pushed at the wedged foot, and we pulled on command. The foot came clear like a cork out of a bottle, and we all fell backwards. The only bad memory of that incident is that I can still feel the sting of the clip around the ear, received from the constable. We never called him 'Flycatcher' again.

(Footnote: Harry Gresty emigrated to Australia, where he now owns an engineering factory.)

Florin Street – Miriam Wells (née Bates)

I was born in 1911 in John Street, Pendleton, in my parents' home opposite the old John Street School, though we later moved to Armitage Street, off Whit Lane. The latter house had a gable end, and was situated near a lamp-post, so it was a favourite playground for the bigger children of the area. A rope thrown over the bar of the lamp-post made a good swing. My older sisters played the piano, so if there was music to be heard, children would squat on the kerb or under the window to listen. There was often a crowd outside the house, as well as inside, for, in addition to my sisters and brother, my parents also brought up my two cousins.

The family eventually left Armitage Street to take a greengrocery shop in Florin Street. Dad continued with his own job, whilst Mum looked after the shop. She had to rise very early to take the tram to Smithfield Market in Manchester. Most of the items she selected would be delivered to the shop later in the day, but she had a special coat in which to carry certain purchases - she would travel home with English rabbits threaded on her belt. Not far away, another greengrocer bought foreign rabbits for her customers, but she always sent for a couple of Mum's English rabbits for her own family. Mum's rabbit pies were certainly delicious - I can visualise them now, in huge brown eathenware dishes, steaming hot and wholesome.

The shop door was on an angle, and there was a large window in Florin Street with another in Boundary Street. When it was market day, the cattle would be driven past our shop. On one occasion a large cow put its head in the doorway and gave a loud 'Moo,' after which Mum always fastened the door when the cattle were passing. One of the benefits of having a shop at that time was in being asked to display posters advertising the various shows or films at local theatres. These were always accompanied by two free tickets, which Mum used to her advantage. The shop sold mineral waters and ices (made in the cellar), and local youths used to buy these. Mum would offer the two free tickets in turn to those who would agree to clean the windows, inside and out.

A Police Sergeant was a regular visitor to the street corner outside the shop, at which point he used to meet his constables. He used to rap with his stick several times on the kerb, a signal for the other officers to meet for further instructions. The first time I heard the noise from his stick, it frightened me, but we became used to its regular occurrence. Dad was woken in the mornings by a 'Knocker Up' called Blind George, who would rattle on the bedroom windows with wires on the end of a pole. He didn't frighten me as much as the Police Sergeant. When he came round to collect his money, he was always dressed in black with a pot (bowler) hat.

When Mum and Dad moved from Florin Street to Hayfield Terrace, we thought we were privileged to have small garden, in which I used to grow marigolds and other little flowers. Mum was very house-proud, and on Sundays, whilst my sisters were polishing the brass stair-rods Mum would be cleaning all the brasses.

I went to school in Fitzwarren Street, but one time contracted Scarlet Fever. My bed was moved into the parlour, and sheets, covering all the furniture and each side of the door, were sprayed with disinfectant. My illness led to our gas supply being cut off! The room had a gas fire, and a gas chandelier, with fancy globes covering the mantles, but, unfortunately, a gas leak was detected in my sick room. Because of the infectious nature of my illness, the leak could not be attended to, and the supply was sealed-off. The family had to manage with oil lamps borrowed from neighbours. Sometimes, when children were passing by the windows of my sickroom, I heard them say, "Don't walk on that side of the street. You'll catch fever."

Disappearing Traditions—Mrs. L. Culshaw

I came to live in Salford in 1946. Some features of everyday life, which were commonplace then, have quietly disappeared over the intevening years.

Where, for example, are the newspaper sellers, who used to walk round the streets selling Sunday's "Empire News" on a Saturday night? And where have all those once-familiar blue police boxes gone? In our area, there was an old lady who used to act as 'knocker-up' in the days before everyone had an alarm clock. She used to be out and about as early as 4.00am, rattling her pole on the bedroom windows of her clients. She was very conscientious, went out in all weathers, and would not stop knocking until the sleepers acknowledged her call. She charged only a few pennies per week, and could not have made much of a living.

Then there were the Whit Walks, and the ritual visits to show off the new clothes. The tradition of buying new clothes for Whitsuntide seems to have vanished. On Whit Sunday, children, often unwillingly, used to be dressed in their finery, and fond mothers would plan the annual round of calling on friends, relatives and neighbours so that their offspring could be seen in their new outfits. There might be a token show of resistance, but an advantage was the increase of pocket-money from the coins collected on the way.

On Whit Monday evening, the churches and chapels of Higher Broughton and Cheetham Hill walked in procession through Cheetham Village to Half Way House, where the scholars from the Salford Sunday Schools used to return to their home base via Leicester Road. The Roman Catholic Schools walked in Manchester on Whit Friday. Sadly, the Whit Walks largely vanished when Whitsun gave way to the Spring Bank Holiday.

Cross Lane in the late 30s and early 40s

Ted Gray

As a child, I came to know Cross Lane well through the twice-daily walk to school. Looking back, there seems to have been a great deal of interest along its length, and, if it was possible, I would like to return to the Cross Lane of 1939, armed with a camera and an unlimited supply of film with which to record some of those features which I took for granted fifty years ago.

Starting from the famous 'grand union' tramway junction at the Ship Hotel corner, where on wet days small boys used to be fascinated by the sudden spouts of water sent up by the working of the tramway's automatic points, there was the Palace Theatre. By 1939 this was mainly a cinema, but still staged the occasional live shows. One of the highlights of my year was the annual pantomime presented by the Salford Police Force; the plot never mattered – the great thing was to see the largest and most ungainly members of the force dressed up as fairies! Just after the war, comedians such as Harry Secombe and Tony Hancock appeared on stage.

On the opposite side of the road, just a few doors away from each other, were two sweetshops, Martin's and Fieldsend's, both of which also competed with each other by running a fleet of motor coaches.

Cross Lane railway station was a source of unending fascination. If you could avoid the eagle eye of the booking clerk in his office at the side, it was possible to step down from the path on to the footbridge spanning the tracks, and look down the staircases to the platforms. With their raised square treads, the steps always reminded me of a giant chocolate bar. I looked at those square treads in September 1939, when, along with others from West Liverpool Street school, I was one of many evacuees being taken from Cross Lane Station to Lancaster, wondering how long it would be before we saw home again.

The station had four main line tracks, with a fifth branching on the Hodge Lane side which led back under Cross Lane giving access to the cattle sidings between there and Liverpool Street. The footbridge was a good spot to collect engine numbers, the walls on Cross Lane road bridge being just a little too high to see over comfortably. The names of the 'Station Hotel' (Alderman Higginbottom, licensee) and the 'Railway Inn' had obvious connections, but the significance of the title 'London & North Western Hotel' on the other side of the bridge escaped me at the time.

At the back of a croft behind and on the far side of the LNWR Hotel, Martin's garaged their coaches in a shed, whilst opposite, between Lord Duncan Street and Woodbine Street, lay the massive barracks of the Lancashire Fusiliers. I envied one of my school friends, Harry McNichol, whose father was the caretaker of the barracks, more usually known as the 'Drill Hall.' The McNichol family had an apartment high on the front of the barracks, overlooking Cross Lane. It was reached from inside the Drill Hall by climbing a long and very steep flight of stairs. Young visitors were not usually welcomed in the barracks, so when I did manage to gain entry in company with Harry, on the excuse of calling at his home, the occasions were to be savoured.

The 'Carlton Cinema' was opened opposite to the barracks just before the Second World War. It was considered superior to the other local cinemas. Whilst waiting for the programme to start, patrons could gaze with admiration at the scene above the proscenium arch – Venice, complete with gondolas. I don't know who chose that particular scene for Salford, but it was very impressive. The 'Carlton' also boasted an organ, which would rise from the pit in front of the stage. Reginald Liversedge, the resident organist, would play selections of popular music for ten minutes or so before the main feature film, and I remember being surprised some years later to find him in a different setting playing classical music in the hall of the Royal Technical College in Peel Park.

Cross Lane about 1946, viewed from a point outside the Palace Cinema, which is under the verandah to the left. Across the station bridge towards Liverpool Street, the tower of the barracks may be noted (centre left), whilst on the right, one of Martin's motor coaches is parked outside his sweetshop. In the centre of the road, a Salford Corporation tramcar, soon to be scrapped, works the Circular Route to Broughton.

Amongst the shopkeepers in the row on the Liverpool Street side of the cinema were Tom Witt, the tailor; Abraham Lazarus, cabinet-maker ; and Tom Goodale, the barber, to whom I was sent to have regular hair-cuts. I hated these visits. For one thing, the waiting time, whilst the barber dealt with the adult customers, seemed interminable to a small boy, and for another, the long bench with the horse-hair upholstery, on which I had to sit, was agonisingly prickly to someone wearing short trousers. The barber's large window on to Cross Lane was almost wholly painted over, or obscured in some way, so it was not possible to relieve the boredom by watching the passing traffic. Only a small top portion of window glass remained clear, and through this one could see a few inches of sky. At intervals, the tedium of waiting would be enlivened by a growing rumble and roar, which signalled the approach of a tramcar on its way to the Docks. Then the whole shop would vibrate, and the top of the trolley-pole would be glimpsed against the skyline as it swished past on the overhead wire.

Opposite to the barber's, on the corner of Woodbine Street, was a branch of Wetherall's grocery chain, a once familiar name in the area, and over the street the chemist's shop of Mr. Emlyn Edwards, a real gentleman. Even as a child, I recognised that Mr. Edwards seemed to embody courtesy, patience and charm, no matter how small or insignificant his customer. Next door to him was my favourite establishment – Tootell's toffee shop, where my 'Saturday penny' was often spent on Cadbury's chocolate caramels.

Beyond Southport Street, near to the Liverpool Street junction, was a block which included the Buck Hotel (Openshaw Brewery) and a newsagent, with a butcher's shop on the corner. This corner shop had a splendid turret-like roof, which always reminded me of a medieval castle. On the other side of the junction was the chemist and photographer Jno. Jones, whose name intrigued me. Was 'Jno' one of those peculiar Welsh names, I wondered? (The name lives on in the Langworthy Road photographic shop run by his son, Peter Jones.)

Further along was Harrold's, the grocer, in rivalry with the Pendleton Co-Operative Industrial Society, more usually known as 'The Stores,' Mack's the tailor, and on the corner of West High Street, the Empire Billiards Hall. For some reason unspecified, billiards halls seemed to have a dubious reputation, and parents instructed their offspring not to go there! So I never saw the inside the the Empire Billiards Hall, but interest revived at a later date when it was taken over by the Lyons Ice Cream Company, presumably for storage purposes. Butting on to the other side of the billiards hall, facing the open market site, was a long, rather ramshackle lean-to structure, which served as a garage for Fieldsend's motor coaches. Whereas Martin's owned only two or three vehicles, Fieldsend's business was a larger concern, with seven or eight coaches, some of which were requisitioned for war purposes. When the garage was empty, two elderly-looking charabancs could be seen amidst the gloom in the far corner. I never saw them in use, and wondered why they never moved. Although at the time they must have been only ten or twelve years old, their body styles from the 1920s marked them out as antiques when compared to the post-1936 design of the rest of the fleet. Much later I learned that the Ministry of War Transport would not permit the disposal of any vehicles, even unserviceable ones, in case of urgent shortages, and I assume they were scrapped when the situation eased in 1945-46.

On the space next to Fieldsend's garage, formerly the main entrance to the cattle market, was sited during the war a 'British Restaurant,' a pre-fabricated single-storey building, established with the aim of providing plain but wholesome food during the period of shortages and rationing. Next to it was the longer-established 'Cattle Market Hotel.' On the opposite side of the road was the 'Cattle Market Tavern,' an entirely separate concern, despite the similar name, and the 'Craven Heifer' hotel, (now 'The Golden Gate'), whose name I never understood. It was notable, however, in having rows of cut-out silhouetted heads placed along the base of the saloon windows, which stuck out starkly when lit from within. I used to wonder why the customers never moved.

The former cattle market site was the venue for the annual visits of the travelling fairground. The roundabouts and steam organs, with their general air of jollity, were an essential part of the festivities at Christmas and Whitsuntide. On one occasion, one of my teenage friends, patronising a shooting-gallery stall and, aiming at a clay pipe, managed to shoot a china plate in the prize display. The stall-holder was not pleased, and ordered us away, refusing further custom from our little crowd.

Beyond lay Unwin Street, leading to Unwin Square, large and open enough to make it a regular destination point for the open-air services which were part of the Whitsun and Anniversary Sunday School processions, the 'Whit Walks.' On the corner, the 'Butcher's Arms' and behind it the Salford Paint and Varnish Works, with the distinctive 'S.P.V.' on its chimney.

Near the end of Cross Lane, opposite the triangle of grass holding the obelisk (and for a time, some underground air raid shelters), was one of our favourite haunts as teenagers - the Salford Hippodrome, later, and quite unnecessarily, re-named the 'Windsor Theatre.'

Beyond the Hippodrome, but set back from the road and fronted by a long garden, was a large house which was the home of 'Hall's Herbal Remedies,' and at the corner of Broad Street was Underwood's radio shop, previously known as 'Jean's Corner.' (How many people remember carrying heavy accumulator batteries to radio shops to be charged up?) Not strictly on Cross Lane, but just a few yards round the corner on Broad Street, was a shop where our teenage strolls often used to end with some modest self-indulgence at Williams' Ice Cream Parlour, where Mr. Williams' two daughters would dispense his delicious ice cream with great charm. A little further on was a sheet-music shop and Krinks' Hairdressing Salon, which I patronised when I was old enough to wander further on my own. The Krinks shop was a much larger establishment than Goodale's, with six or more barbers' chairs, and by not having horse-hair sofas, recommended itself to me. An advertisement in the shop was always a source of amusement for our English teacher - *"How Does Krinks Cut Your Hair ? As You Like It (Shakespeare)."*

A 1948 view of Cross Lane shows smooth tarmac covering the abandoned tram rails in the centre of the road, though setts remain on either side. On the left is the "Cattle Market Hotel," facing the "Cattle Market Tavern" on the right. The 'modernistic' clock tower of 1939 marks the entrance to the open air market, on the site of the old cattle market. Beyond the clock is the "Butcher's Arms" public house on the corner of Unwin Street, the chimney of the Salford Paint & Varnish Works, the Salford Hippodrome, and, at the junction with Broad Street, Bradford's engineering works.

Cross Lane

remembered by Lilian Swanwick

Cross Lane was famous for all its ale-houses,
And shops that sold frocks, and men's baggy trousers.
Pawnshops, chip shops, and good theatres, too,
And some, like the pot-shops, that sold dolly blue.
Fred Oddie, the butcher, with a good sausage trade,
And a barracks nearby, where soldiers were made.
There were bicycles, handcarts, and tramcars with bells,
And the market, of course, with linoleum smells,
Lucketti's hot potatoes, and ice cream in tubs,
But the best of Cross Lane was its piano'd pubs.

Christmas Food Collection

Don Rainger

The Salford Companionship Circle for the Elderly was founded in 1955 in co-operation with the Welfare Department. One of its aims was to ensure that each of the 4000 persons living alone was visited at least once every six months. I joined the Circle in 1963, at the age of 14, when I was impressed by an appeal to the boys at Salford Grammar school for helpers during 'Salford Food Week.' This was a house-to-house collection of food items, which were later sorted and boxed before being distributed to the elderly at Christmas time.

My Housemaster put my name down, and soon I was delivering leaflets in the Lancaster Road area to prepare residents for the forthcoming collection. The next year, now a house prefect, I was upgraded and placed in charge of a number school friends who were acting as volunteer collectors. Members of staff from school provided the cars necessary for trans-porting the food. The base for our collecting area was the Oakwood Hotel, where the kindly landlord allowed us use of the spacious entrance hall as a temporary collection point. On the actual evening of the collection in 1964, his kindness was more than usually appreciated, as there was a tremendous hail-storm, and boys were staggering in, covered in white, bowed low with sacks of tinned food, etc. The following year, we estimated that some $2\frac{1}{2}$ tons of food were collected during these evenings, requiring three van trips to the Civic Welfare Office.

In remember 1965 well because of the dense fog. My number 25 bus took hours to reach the Oakwood. Although most of our task had already been accomplished, there remained a few roads to visit in order to complete the collection, and the band of helpers set off with the usual enthusiasm. My road was Welwyn Drive, which led to the Swinton Park Golf Course. The fog swirled and grew more dense, as I groped for garden gates. Even though I carried a torch, I could see nothing. Shouting to the other collectors produced no result. I wandered lost for some fifteen minutes before I realised that I was actually on the golf course. Eventually, I reached a road collected a bag full of food, and found my way back to the safety of the Oakwood Hotel, where an anxious teacher was relieved to see me.

My final food collection was in 1966, this time assisted by girls from Pendleton High School. We distributed some 4000 leaflets and collected $13\frac{1}{2}$ tea chests full of food. A reward came in the shape of an invitation to join other school representatives at a tea party hosted by the Mayor in the Town Hall. Looking back, the features which remain in the mind are the pleasant comradeship, the enthusiasm, the dreadful weather, frozen fingers, overloaded cars, the generosity of the house-holders, and, of course, the obvious pleasure of those who received the parcels on distribution night. The green and gold blazer was a welcome sight to those who were contemplating a frugal Christmas dinner.

The Errand Boy

Bill Fereday

I couldn't wait for Saturday mornings. If I was lucky, I could earn seven shillings and sixpence, about 36p in today's money. I was seven or eight years old at the time, so it would be around 1955. I lived in Phoebe Street, Salford, with my Mam and Dad, two older brothers (Tony and Alan), and younger brother (Joe) and sister (Linda). In our household there was always a shortage of money, so we rarely got any spends. Running errands for anybody who would trust me, gave me the chance to earn some 'picture money' or 'toffee money.'

I remember in particular a Mrs. Jarvis, who lived almost opposite our house. I would knock on her door and disturb her rest quite early on a Saturday morning. She must have been quite annoyed at times, but she never showed it. She was very kind. I knew I would be given at least half-a-crown (12$\frac{1}{2}$p in today's money). She would make a list of the 'rations' she needed - bread, barm cakes, and fancy cakes from Armistead's pie shop, general groceries from 'The Meadow Dairy,' and meat from Wade Woods, the butcher, all of which were in Tatton Street. Armistead's was one of my favourite shops. I always asked for a bag of broken cakes, and I was never refused. A lovely, kindly lady called May would give them to me - she had a nice, warm smile, and I've never forgotten her. When shopping for groceries in 'The Meadow,' I would ask for broken biscuits, and, again, was never refused. I cannot remember the man's name, but he had a kind face. He was tall, with silver hair, and wore a white button-up overall, always very

tidy. In Wade Woods butcher's shop, the manager, called Eddie, used to give me a bag of sausage meat, which I ate with my fingers out of the bag. It was great ! Eddie was always smiling, and his customers loved him.

After eating several broken cakes and biscuits, and some sausage meat, I would feel bloated, and take the rest home for the family to share. Sometimes, after leaving the butcher's shop, I would walk up Phoebe Street in the direction of Regent Road, where there was a 'Spud Shop,' Payne's, on the corner of New Bury Street. It had three steps leading up into the shop, which made it hard work if you were carrying bags of meat and groceries and had to collect a heavy bag of fruit and vegetables as well. It always seemed especially difficult in bad weather, when it was 'tippling down.' I think the shop assistants in Payne's must have felt sorry for me, because, without having to ask, I was usually given a free apple or pear.

I would struggle back to Mrs. Jarvis and pick up my half-crown. I used to love that. Sometimes I would polish it with 'Duraglit' to make it shine. My next stop would be Mrs. Young in Tamworth Street, who usually just needed something from the corner shop, so I might get only a threepenny-bit or a sixpence, but it all mounted up.

Mrs. Metcalfe (Kitty) would send me to Hugh & Fay Ltd., in Tatton Street. It was always a bit 'posh' in there. There was always a big queue, and everything was a bit more expensive than in the other shops, but Kitty would want nice, lean bacon, the best cheese and fresh eggs. She would give me at least two shillings (10p today). We lived only a few doors away from Kitty, so I ran errands quite a lot for her. She would pay me, and say, "There's your picture money. Don't lose it down a grid!"

My next stop, usually my last, was at Mrs. Hunter's in Phoebe Street. This always meant a trip to Whitworth's Coal Yard in Robert Hall Street, and many's the time I have queued on the cobblestones in that yard, often in the cold and rain, waiting to pay at a little sliding hatch in the office wall. My head would just about reach the required level, and when the hatch opened, the lovely warm air from inside would bathe my frozen face, and the

Errand boy Bill Fereday and a tin badge which was once worn with pride by those lucky enough to attend the Salford Poor Children's Holiday Camp. Nowadays, the title would be con-demned as a mark of disgrace.

smell of pipe tobacco would drift out into the cold air. I would ask for half a hundredweight of coal, hand in the money, and receive in exchange a slip of paper to present to the weighman. He would shovel the coal into a large scoop attached to the scales, then, if I was lucky, empty it into a small hand-drawn coal truck which he allowed me to borrow to make the delivery. If I was unlucky, and if I hadn't turned up with my own pram or makeshift bogie, the coal went into a hessian sack, which I would have to carry on my back. It was very hard work, and I've had to carry a few bags in my time.

There was also a coke yard in Robert Hall Street, called Millington's, where a great big man, always wearing a black beret on his head, would serve me. I think his name was Claud. I don't ever remember him speaking – he was just a big, quiet man. After taking the coal to Mrs. Hunter's house, and dropping it down through her cellar grid. I would collect my two shillings, or whatever she could afford, and run home. I would give my Mam some of the money, wash the coal dust off my hands, and then call for my best mate, 'Vinny,' who lived only a few doors away. Together we would decide which picture house to go to. Often, it was the Kings on Regent Road, sometimes known as 'The Bug Hut.' Happy days!

I loved all those streets and shops, where I spent so much of my time. Favourite places for my own shopping included Jack's on Tatton Street, for 'Vimto' lollies ; the 'Dinky Chip Shop' for the best pennyworth of 'scratchings' in the world ; the U.C.P. tripe shop for 'savoury ducks'; McKintyre's, in Phoebe Street, for 'snake belts,' laces, pumps and bumpers; Johnny's chip shop (he was never mean, and always gave plenty); Watson's pie shop (now they were really pies); and the 'Pot Shop' with a ghost in the cellar, or was it a White Lady?

Now, I take my grandson around the City of Salford, and tell him about my past and the days gone by.

Evacuation (1939) and 'Trickle Evacuation' (1941)

Winifred Birchall

At the outbreak of the 1939-45 War, because of the feared danger from enemy air raids, it was Government policy to evacuate all children of school age from large urban areas. If their parents were agreeable, the children were to be removed to places of comparative safety. Consequently, in September 1939 this policy was put into effect in Salford. Naturally, the schools and teachers played a major part in the scheme. It was their form of war work.

At the time, I was a young teacher serving at the Langworthy Road Infants' School, and I moved with the children of that school to Blackpool. Other schools were moved to different parts of the county. None of us knew what to expect. It must have been a traumatic time for parents who made the decision to say "Goodbye" to their children, not knowing if or when they would see them again; and for the children to go to strange places to live with strange people. As for we teachers, we were so busy looking after our charges that we had little time to grieve.

But, in the event, this proved to be the period of the 'Phoney War.' There was no enemy action in this region for several months, and gradually, as fears were forgotten, parents began to take their children home, until, at last, there were sufficient numbers back in Salford to justify the reopening of schools, and the return of most of the staff to work in them. Some children remained away from home, of course, but, in the main, these were the ones who were settled and happy with their foster parents, and who became integrated into the local community in the area of their new homes.

Back in Salford, school life went on much as before, except there were walls of sand-bags at all the entrances, sticky strips across windows, and frequent Air Raid Drills, which meant moving (complete with registers) down to the basement. These happened whenever the air raid warning sirens sounded, and we became quite expert at nipping up and down cellar steps. We sang interminable songs whilst down below.

Our meagre resources of materials had to be conserved carefully. In the Infants' School we used small blackboards and chalk for all rough writing in order to save paper. We painted on newspaper and did handwork with waste materials – cotton reels, toilet roll centres, etc. We settled into this routine and into general tightening of belts. We heard and read of severe air raids in other parts of the country, particularly London, but our turn did not come until December 1940 – Christmas week.

The calamity of the Christmas Blitz has been well-documented elsewhere. Suffice to say here

Salford children assemble in their school playground for the first wave of evacuation in September 1939. All are tagged with labels, and carry their limited belongings in sacks or pillow-cases, ready to be led to the railway station and an unknown destination.

that, when the tumult had subsided, many parents asked the Local Education Authority to arrange for their children to return to safer zones. Names were collected at the Education Office, and groups of children from various schools were sent off in charge of an assortment of teachers, also from various schools. They went, as the numbers and accommodation required, in batches of 40 to 50 at a time. This was known as 'Trickle Evacuation.'

Consequently, on a cold winter's afternoon in February 1941, I found myself on the platform of Seedley Station, then on Langworthy Road, with two other young teachers, Evelyn and Dilys. This was the first time we had met. There was an assortment of children and some parents on the station, together with a harassed official from the Education Office, who was reading names from a list. There should have been two children from Langworthy Road, but they had not come. I said perkily, "Oh, I can go home then." The official replied sternly, "It is your national duty to go." I was squashed! Looking back, I feel sorry for him – he had an unpleasant and frustrating task.

When the train arrived and we all piled in, there were 40 children from 14 different schools. The oldest was a boy, Albert, aged 14, school-leaving age in those days, whilst the youngest was a little girl of three. I knew none of them. Evelyn had two from her school, Hope Street, and Dilys three from hers, Halton Bank. All the others were strangers to us and to one another - what a pickle ! We had no idea where we were going, and when we asked, were not told. 'Careless talk costs lives,' was the motto of the day, though what interest our little band would be to the enemy, I could not comprehend.

After a long and weary journey, during which it became dark (in wartime, that meant a 'blacked-out' train, with each carriage lit by only a single, small blue lamp-bulb), we arrived at Knott End, on the opposite side of the estuary from Fleetwood, in a snowstorm. We were met by the Reception Officer of the Local Council, Roger by name. He escorted us to a hall, where some very apprehensive local residents were waiting. They began to bid for the children, as in an auction. "I'll have that little girl." "I don't want a boy." "I can't take two." So it went on, until all the children were placed.

Dilys had a family friend in the area, so she was all right for a billet. Evelyn and I were left till last, and had to share not only a room, but also a double-bed, in a rather run-down boarding house. No wonder we became good friends! We were wakened early the next morning by Roger, who informed us that Albert (the 14-year-old) had disappeared from his billet during the night. We went out to look for him – a waste of time, as we couldn't even remember what he looked like. He never returned to us – we learnt later that he had 'hitched' his way back to Salford.

We were given the local 'British Legion' hut for a school building. It was a wooden structure, with a stage, a piano of sorts, a few chairs and benches, and nothing else. We had no school supplies of any sort from Salford. Being the oldest of the three teachers, I was invited to take charge. On the first day, we had a long concert, 9.00am to 4.30pm, interspersed with playtimes. Luckily for us, the children went 'home' for dinner. I visited the local school and borrowed a blackboard and easel, some pencils and paper, and a few books for the older ones, to tide us over. We made three classes – Senior, Junior, and Infant – which fortunately co-incided with our teaching skills. Evelyn took the Seniors, Dilys the Juniors, and I the Infants. The little ones went home half-an-hour before the others, as in Salford, and in that time I did the clerical work and kept in touch with the children's Salford schools.

On the first weekend after our arrival, I returned to Salford to see the new Director of Education, F. A. J. Rivett, and asked for supplies. Some days later, a van containing basic supplies arrived, and we were able to repay the local school and settle down to a regular routine. It was amazing how quickly this happened, and how happy we became in our little school. We were thrilled to be congratulated on our work by a visiting Government Inspector.

All the children settled in with their foster parents. These were, in the main, country folk, who made the children part of their family. (Some children stayed on at the end of the war.) The foster parents did not seem to either want or expect us to visit the billets at night, as we had done in Blackpool. This meant that, after we had done our normal schoolwork and preparation for the following day, our evenings were free.

At home, my wartime commitments had left me little free time. I was involved with the A.R.P.; the Civil Nursing Reserve (two evenings per week on duty at Hope Hospital from close of school until 8.30pm) ; and a Youth Club in South Salford (two evenings per week). The enforced halt from these activities gave me a holiday feeling, in spite of the reason for our stay. We saw little of the war in Knott End. Just one night we could hear the bombs dropping on Barrow, across Morecambe Bay, and see the fires which ensued.

We three teachers stayed for three months, after which time the Education Authority had worked out a regular monthly rota for staff replacement from home. A good communal billet for the teachers had been found, and I believe that life went smoothly. On my return to Salford, I was appointed to the staff of the newly-opened Lancaster Road School (now Lightoaks), so I came off the Knott End rota. 'Trickle Evacuation,' to me, proved to be fun while it lasted. What it is to be young!

The driver of a Salford tramcar rests on his controls and looks on sadly, as evacuees from the Adelphi area cross The Crescent on their way to join trains at Ordsall Station on 1st. September, 1939.

'Fairhope'

Rita A. Faulkner

'Fairhope' was one of the last privately-owned estates on the Pendleton 'Millionaires' Mile', and whilst there were several houses on the estate, the largest was owned by the Prestwich family, of the Protector Lamp Company, Lansdowne Road, Monton. Mr. and Mrs. Prestwich, with their children John and Nancy, lived in the 'Big House.' The Agnew and Mills families lived in two more, and Mrs. Bowen and her son lived in the Lodge. A working farm at the end of the long driveway had an exit into Guildford Road, which proved very useful to my brother and myself, for one of our regular chores took us that way very often.

My father became a motor engineer after 'serving his time' as a toolmaker at G.E.C., and then repairing lorries and tanks in the 1914-18 War. The garage in Weaste where he worked was scheduled to close, but he was offered work by many of the customers. As this was in the late 1920s, the people who owned the cars were mainly the wealthy local residents. So, he rented the Coach House at Fairhope, a long building, with huge and beautiful sliding doors, and a deep, white, tile-lined pit for working underneath vehicles. (There were no hydraulic ramps at that time.) Horse-drawn coaches had been housed and maintained in this building, and there was also a glass-covered courtyard, called 'The Wash,' where we did the 'valeting.' About eight cars could be parked under cover here. The long wall inside the garage had a workbench and huge battery-charging equipment. Alongside was a row of carboys, containing acid, from which the 'wet batteries' were topped-up by means of a large pipette. After topping-up, the batteries were connected by large 'dog clips' to meters for an overnight trickle charge.

My brother and I would occasionally collect and deliver batteries for customers who wanted them charged for use with their radio sets. Trouble ensued if we tilted the batteries and spilt acid on our socks and shoes.

My father worked on some beautiful cars, and I was sometimes told not to breathe whilst he separated sheets of gold leaf, thinner than tissue paper, with which he embellished the paint-work of a Rolls Royce. When repainting a car, he would spray and rub-down about six times, so that it polished up like new. He had a compressor for the spray gun, which had a fat end about two feet high, and looked as though it was a 'Michelin man' sitting on the front, vibrating up and down. The 'Michelin man' went to help the war effort in 1939 when scrap metal was needed, and with his departure, I lost interest in the compressor.

Next to the garage, the estate stables were rented by Mr. Hamyl, whose young sons and daughter carried out their tasks of brushing, curry-combing, and feeding the beautiful horses he used for riding lessons on the Paddock, which was a large field on the other side of the estate road. Mr. Hamyl organised gymkanas on the field at the top of Stott Lane, and one year George Formby and his wife Beryl attended. Beryl had an accident, and I remember that the triangular fruit ices from the Walls 'Stop Me And

Buy One' tricycle were used to ease her bump.

We seldom saw the house-owners on the estate, but sometimes I went up to the farm to collect a rare treat of fresh cream. Unfortunately, I lost that job when the farmer's wife informed my mother that she had seen me lift the cardboard lid of the carton and have a 'swig.' She could see a long way down the drive because it was so straight!

We children were invited to the November 5th bonfires on the estate, always a big thrill for us. Pea soup and parkin were provided, together with roasted chestnuts from the farm's coal oven. The fire in the oven was huge, and one year a stray spark set off some fireworks which had been stored in a big wicker basket. We ran for our lives as rockets, pin-wheels, and bangers took light and shot in every direction. On another occasion, a young man was larking about with a girl guest, picking her up and pretending to throw her on the bonfire as a 'guy.' He tripped, and dropped her on the edge of the fire. After that, Mum said the young people were too lively for us, and we saw no more bonfires.

During the 1939-45 war, parts of the estate, including the stables and garage, were taken over by the army, and as Dad was called up to work at the Royal Ordnance Factory, he settled for just running a taxi and doing occasional work in a small garage. Our connection with Fairhope was nearly over, but we were invited to the ENSA concerts, which were usually held in a tent or a Nissen hut. They included some bawdy humour, but also some lovely music. After the war, the estate was purchased by the Salford Council and the present housing estate was built.

I can still see Walter Greenwood, shortly after his success with 'Love On The Dole,' sitting on a fallen gate-post by the side of the garage, with his typewriter on another stone, busily working away whilst waiting for Dad to finish repairing his car.

Fairhope House in 1917, when it was in use as a temporary military hospital.

Garden Lane Childhood

Alan James Jennings

I was born under a November sky in 1946 in that part of old Salford which formed the triangle made up of Gravel Lane, Greengate, and Blackfriars Road. I came into the world in Artisans' Dwellings, but soon we moved the few yards to 25 Garden Lane, opposite the door of the 'snug' of 'The Three Crowns' public house, where my mother spent many hours, both as a cleaner and customer. This old pub still stands today, though now re-named 'The Buskers.' Why was Garden Lane so named? There were certainly no gardens when I was born, but perhaps there had been in the distant past. Also in the lane were two other taverns, the 'Mechanics' and 'The Star', and just across the road was the 'Blackfriars' pub.

My mother had left her first husband to live with my father George Jennings when she was expecting my sister Doreen, who was born on the 8th June 1945. Then came me, followed by my younger sister Brenda in 1948, and brother Roy in 1951. We lived a life of poverty which seems unreal today. Our house was a two-up, two-down, with attic and cellar, and was in a poor state of repair, having been built in the early years of the nineteenth century. For lighting, we had only a gas mantle in the front room where we lived and ate. In the rest of the house, we relied upon an oil lamp and candles. We all slept in the front bedroom – father, brother and myself in one bed, my mother and sisters in another. Having no blankets, the beds were covered with old overcoats, and were full of bugs. Our toilet was outside in the communal yard, shared with our neighbours. There was no hot water tap, and no sink save for an old 'slopstone.'

Our family doctor was Dr. Joseph Schlosberg, who became Mayor of Salford, and it was he who in the winter of 1952 diagnosed that I had contracted tuberculosis, then a dreaded disease. I can remember standing against the backyard wall of 'The Three Crowns' watching the bonfire on the croft in Hodson Street. It was dark and raining, and everything seemed so far away. I awoke to find myself lying in the front room of our house. Dr. Schlosberg was there, and arranged for my immediate admission to Hope Hospital. I was still there when Queen Elizabeth was crowned in June 1953, but I was allowed a visit home for the Coronation. It was strange to see the houses and shops decked with flags and bunting. I was six years of age by then, and had been away for so long that my brothers and sisters seemed like strangers. I was allowed home for that one day only, and afterwards was sent to a convalescent home in Southport.

Later, instead of returning to my old school, Sacred Trinity, I was sent with my sister Doreen to Claremont Open Air School. On Sundays, we attended Sacred Trinity Church, where our Rector was that wonderful man Canon R.L. Hussey. He was Rector of Sacred Trinity from 1931 to 1962; in 1963 he was made a Freeman of the city. His two sisters, Miss Daisy Hussey and Mrs. Florence Abbs, took our Sunday School classes. They would bring second-hand clothes and toys to our home, and when I was in hospital, Canon Hussey brought me fruit and books to read.

One vivid memory I have is of arriving in church one Sunday when the service had already begun, and sidling into one of the back pews. I heard Canon Hussey asking the congregation to pray for me, as I was very poorly and might be dying in hospital. I wanted to jump up and shout, "I'm here."

Another event in my young life was the filming in our district of the outdoor scenes for "Hobson's Choice" in 1953. I watched as the crew filmed the piece where Maggie confronts Ada Figgins and her mother at the door of their house.

Is there anyone who remembers the ghost in the 'Brazier's Arms?' On one occasion, friends came knocking for us to go urgently to see this phenomenon. The story was that a barmaid, collecting glasses, was suddenly confronted by the vision of a lady in white, hovering in the air. This was alleged to be because a church window had been fitted in the pub in replacement of one which had been broken. We stood outside the pub, where a large crowd had gathered hoping to see the vision. Even the police were present, and officers had placed a rope barrier across the pavement in front of the particular window which was causing all the excitement.

Like Garden Lane, nothing much remains of Hodson Street, but the pub is still there. Also on that side of Blackfriars Road was part of King Street, where was situated Jackie Winders' shop, which stocked oilcloth, rugs, and other items. Mr. Winders once stood as a Conservative candidate in the local elections, and I was amongst a crowd of children who were lifted into the back of a lorry to sing at maximum volume, "Vote, Vote, Vote For Jackie Winders, He is sure to win the day." Whether he did or not, I do not know.

Whit Week was a wonderful time for children. It was the only time of the year when we were given new clothes. It did not matter that immediately afterwards they were taken to May's pawnshop on the corner of Queen Street. It was still a very special time. All the churches took part in the 'Walks,' Church of England on the Monday, Catholics on the Friday. On the Friday, my parents would take us to watch the Catholic walks. We would stand near the old hen market on Shudehill, and I always thought that the Catholic procession was more exotic than ours. Mam and Dad would look forward especially to seeing the Italians, with the men carrying a statue of the Madonna.

Our new shoes were provided free of charge from the Education Offices on Chapel Street. The boys were issued with boots, whilst the girls had black patent leather shoes. It was years before I managed to get my first 'low quarters,' which was the term we used for normal shoes, rather than boots.

In Peel Park Museum's Larkhill Place is an example of a working class home very similar to the one in which I grew up in Garden Lane – but ours was without the tablecloths, rugs, and pictures on the wall. I have so many memories of that old lane – of visits from my half-brothers, Eddie and Kenny. Eddie became a Paratrooper, and served in Egypt during the Suez crisis. He was my hero – he promised to bring home a camel for me. In later years, I often reminded him about his failure to keep this promise, and, eventually, nearly 40 years late, he finally presented me with a camel – a toy one!

Other vivid memories are of my first days at Sacred Trinity School; of our friends and neighbours the Gallaghers, Warings, Swarbricks, Freemans, Bradleys; the lamplighters who walked round the streets lighting the gas lamps; the knockers-up; Kitchingman's sweet shop; Mary's café; and Cecil Suitor's barber-shop. The old Salford I knew and loved is now gone, but I keep a videotape of the "Hobson's Choice" film on which I can see again some of the old streets where I lived. My pleasant semi-detached house in Prestwich is very different, but I do not forget my Salford roots.

'Gerrin, it's Rat Week'

_____ *Roy Bullock*

"Gerrin, it's Rat Week," was a phrase in general use during my boyhood. It was usually the final insult in a verbal altercation with a contemporary. Translated mildly, it meant "Oh, go away." Even at its worst, it was less offensive than some of the insults and words of today.

As a youngster, I was not aware that there had actually been a 'Rat Week,' but it seems it was an annual affair, and not only in Salford. In fact, in the 1930s the first week in November was designated 'National Rat Week,' in an attempt to concentrate attention on the need to wage war on 'ravaging rodents.' The publicity claimed that there were more rats than people in England, and that their presence was a grave menace to health. The rats were said to be the worst carriers of disease, and the authorities called for a 'war of extermination' against these pests.

In Salford, leaflets were distributed to all homes, and posters were displayed in shops and offices, urging everyone to join the fray. It was explained that the first week in November had been chosen for the campaign because it was at this time, when the rodents were migrating in the search for warmer winter quarters, that they could best be caught. However, it was also emphasised that Salford's two professional rat-catchers were employed by the Cleansing Department all the year round, and would be happy to clear premises of vermin, free of charge.

The leaflet explained, "The most common type of rat found in the city is the domestic species, which is greyish-brown in colour. A fully-grown one can weigh anything up to two pounds. It can breed most prolifically, and during twelve months can be responsible for as many as a hundred descendants. Wherever they can find food, they will stay. Shopkeepers and householders are urged to help in preventing rat-breeding by constantly seeing that no foodstuffs are available for the vermin." Advice followed on how best to catch a rat. Poison with a delayed action was recommended, because, it was claimed, the cunning rodents often 'tested' foodstuff by making a young or very old rat eat it. If the 'tester' died, the others would leave the food untouched, but if it appeared to survive, the others would join the feast. 'Nipper traps' placed at the entrance to runs, were also effective.

Salford's professional rat-catchers made 6581 visits to premises in 1936, and 1871 live rats were caught. In many cases, it was found that structural repairs to property were necessary due to the damage done by the rats to fittings and floors. Infestation was often due to faulty or disused drains, which, when reported by the rat-catchers, were corrected and repaired. A Cleansing Department spokesman said, "We regard this as a most important part of our work. I want to appeal to Salford residents to help exterminate rats, and the Department will willingly attend to any inquiries or visit premises where rats are suspected." This was a regular part of the campaign for better Public Health, an aspect which is now all but forgotten.

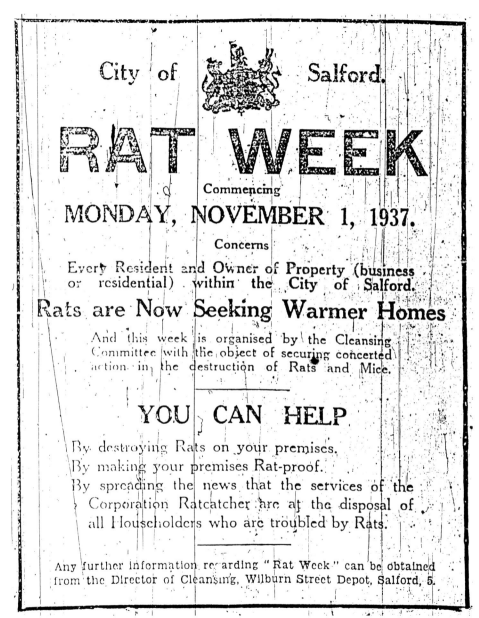

City of Salford

RAT WEEK

Commencing

MONDAY, NOVEMBER 1, 1937.

Concerns

Every Resident and Owner of Property (business or residential) within the City of Salford.

Rats are Now Seeking Warmer Homes

And this week is organised by the Cleansing Committee with the object of securing concerted action in the destruction of Rats and Mice.

YOU CAN HELP

By destroying Rats on your premises.

By making your premises Rat-proof.

By spreading the news that the services of the Corporation Ratcatcher are at the disposal of all Householders who are troubled by Rats.

Any further information regarding "Rat Week" can be obtained from the Director of Cleansing, Wilburn Street Depot, Salford, 5.

A notice from the 'Salford Reporter' announcing the details of the 1937 'Rat Week.'

'Gone to the Dogs'

Joyce Landers

Until a friend asked me whether I would like a part-time job on The Tote at the Albion Greyhound Racing Stadium, I was not aware that such a racetrack existed in Salford. It opened up a whole new world for me. After a couple of weeks training, I began to enjoy it, and it became a pleasure to work alongside my colleagues. Many of the girls working the Tote in the evenings had full-time day jobs as well; for those of us who were housewives, it was just like a night out.

On summer nights, the crowds would come rolling in, and it would remind me of a Lowry scene - young, old, middle-aged, labourers, shop-keepers, business, publicans, etc., all with the one aim of getting the better of the book-makers or the Tote. For many, it was a social occasion. The merits of the dogs were discussed along with family life, politics, or whatever. Most did not wager a great deal of money. Sometimes, crews from ships berthed at the Docks would find their way to the racetrack –most nationalities like a gamble. Often sports celebrities came. Malcolm Allison was a favourite with the girls, and other regular visitors were Pat Crerand, Alex Murphy, and Alan Ball. Alan Ball would stand on the terraces hopping from one foot to the other, never still. Another Salford character was Amy Crossley, who for decades owned a second-hand furniture shop on Chapel Street.

Occasionally, television personalities appeared. A young actor named Richard Beckinsale (then newly-famous in a series called 'The Lovers') attended once, and a complete film crew came to record an episode of 'Coronation Street,' in which 'Alf Roberts' (Bryan Mosley) was the unlikely owner of a greyhound. The television people brought their own dog.

After a few years, I moved into the racing office, which brought me into contact with the racing staff and the greyhounds. Apart from when chasing the mechanical hare, the dogs were usually docile and obedient. Before the racing began, it was part of my job to weigh the dogs and check their ear markings. The dogs would look at me with their soft brown eyes and nuzzle my hand – they were real softies, and very trusting. They made lovely pets, but were not considered to be as glamorous as some other breeds. It is tragic that so many of them have such a short life.

The kennel boys and girls were devoted to the dogs in their charge. The pay for this job was ridiculously low, but the staff turned out seven days a week, in all weathers, to feed and exercise the dogs. Even on Bank Holidays, the staff attended. Perhaps the exercise did them as much good as the dogs. It was a daily ritual to watch the boys and girls, each leading three or four greyhounds, march around the track at exercise time. I often see one former kennel boy, John, now a midddle-aged man, walking round Swinton with one or two dogs by his side.

When in the Judging Box on racing nights, I used to be fascinated by the 'Tick-Tack' men with their white gloves sending messages to bookies on the other side of the track. To this day, I am no

OFFICIAL PROGRAMME   Right to admission strictly reserved.   PRICE 8r

THE ALBION STADIUM — SALFORD
ALBION GREYHOUNDS (Salford) LTD.   Telephone: 782-1918, 1919
(Under the Rules of and licensed by the National Greyhound Racing Club)

44th MEETING
Forty-Ninth Season

FRIDAY JULY 30th, 1976

FIRST RACE 7-30 p.m.   EIGHT RACES

STEWARDS
Mr. E. R. GANLY, Mrs. J. LANDERS, Miss C. HODGKISS, Mr. W. WILEMAN
Judge: Mr. J. I. BHATTY.
Starter: Mr. L. MOORE.
Veterinary Surgeon: Mr. P. NUTT, B.V.M.S., M.R.C.V.S.
General Manager: Mr. E. R. GANLY.
Racing Manager: Mrs. J. LANDERS.
Timekeeper: Mr W. WILEMAN

ABANDONED MEETINGS — In the event of an abandoned meeting retain this Race Card. If owing to any circumstances whatever, it be decided to abandon the Meeting before the Fourth Race has been completed, Patrons will be admitted Free to one of the Three following Meetings on production of the Race Card of the abandoned Meeting.

UNDER NO CIRCUMSTANCES CAN ANY MONEY BE REFUNDED

INQUIRY — Should the Stewards delay in reaching a decision 'INQUIRY' will be announced.

NO RACE — In the event of a NO RACE a Red Light will be shown on the Indicator Board. It is of the utmost importance that once the Red Light is displayed, Totalisator Tickets are not destroyed.

ALL TOTALISATOR TICKETS in a NO RACE must be refunded or exchanged; they will not be valid for RE-RUN Race.

Totalisator tickets will only be paid out on the order of finishing on the Indicator Board accompanied by a Green Light.

Please check your Tote Tickets before leaving tote windows

No result is final until the Green Light appears.

PHOTO FINISH — THE JUDGE'S DECISION IS FINAL.

The judge may call for a photo finish at any time. When a print has been called for copies of the print will be displayed at suitable points in the Stadium

If the judge does not call for a print no print will be made. In the event of a judge calling for a print and no print being available through any unforseen causes, announcement will be made over the loudspeaker.

The Photo Finish Camera has been introduced to help the judge. He will decide the order of finish of the race; the photo finish print may be called for to confirm this decision meanwhile the letter 'P' will be shown on the Indicator Board until the judge has confirmed the final placings. The greyhound whose NOSE first reaches the winning line shall be declared the winner

RESERVE — Reserve will run from Trap of any greyhound withdrawn. The letter 'R' will be shown on the Indicator Board.

THE TRAP POSITIONS have been allocated by the Racing Manager in accordance with Rule 76.

WEIGHTS OF EACH GREYHOUND — appear in parentheses after each performance.

AUTOMATIC START IN OPERATION.

ENCLOSURE   40p   (incl. Programme and V.A.T.)

---

wiser as to what their signals meant, but I suppose that was the idea – no secrets given away.

One night, in the middle of a race, a freak wind blew the roof from one of the stands. Staff could not stand up against the force of the wind, and the meeting had to be abandoned. On my way home, when I reached Irlams O'Th' Height, the wind was so strong it lifted up my 1100 car, and put it down on the opposite side of the road, fortunately with no ill-effects.

One councillor in particular was intent on closing the racetrack, and eventually a compulsory purchase order was served. The stadium closed in 1976. I wonder what jobs the racing staff were able to find after the closure, for many of them had known no other kind of work. Some of the bookies asked for keepsakes of the old track to remind them of Salford, and Manager E.R. Ganley gave one of them an old-fashioned coat-rack. I have one of the seats which stood on the track for the 50 years of its existence. Repainted and restored, it looks quite nice in my garden, and it is hard to imagine that it is 66 years old. I also have my stop-watch to remind me of the interesting and pleasant time I worked there.

A cover of a 1976 programme for the Albion Stadium in the final season of greyhound racing. The writer's name may be noted as both Steward and Racing Manager.

'Hanky Park' Characters of the 1920s

As remembered by Margaret Finlay

Map of the 'Hanky Park' area of Pendleton in the 1920s. Pendleton Church is top centre, and Hankinson Street runs down the centre of the map.

'Hanky Park' was the area around Hankinson Street, Pendleton, made famous in the writings of Walter Greenwood. I was born in 1912, and my family lived in Earl Street, which lay between Tanners Lane and Hankinson Street.

Walter Greenwood himself lived in Rossall Street, which had rather a bad name. It was regarded as 'rough,' and was noted for frequent fights. Greenwood was seen as a socialist agitator. He would hold political meetings in the district. People would say, "He's on his soap box again." During the cotton strike, he appeared with a barrel organ, attracting attention and collecting funds.

Miss Hutton was the Headmistress of Primrose Hill School, which was for girls only. The boys attended Hankinson Street School. On one occasion, my school's badge, bearing the letters P.H.S., was a source of confusion when a complaint was made about a girl's behaviour outside school, and it was assumed that she was a Primrose Hill scholar. Miss Hutton, in directing the critic to the correct source of the misdeed, said haughtily, "My girls are far superior to the Pendleton High School girls."

'Father' Peter Burns, at his shop at 56 Hankinson Street, was well-known for his willingness to sell small quantities, such as a pennyworth of treacle or jam. Shop-keeper Lizzie Hughes, at number 51, had a side-line as a 'layer-out' of corpses. Lizzie Pickup made large quantities of hot-pot in her washing boiler, and would sell small portions. On Sundays, she made barm cakes in her old oven.

Walter Greenwood, author of 'Love On The Dole,' wrote about life in 'Hanky Park.' In his youth he lived in Rossall Street. He is seen here in 1973, re-visiting the area during its re-development.

Regular visitors to the district included Dr. Hewlett Johnson, the 'Red Dean,' during his time at Manchester Cathedral, and Jimmy Miller, who became 'Ewan McColl' the folk-singer, and who attended the Fletchers' political meetings, and played their harmonium. Miller's father worked at Hodgkinson's foundry at Pendleton. When my father was incapacitated, Mr. Davies used to call bringing a shilling every week from the Oddfellows Society, but a less-welcome visitor was Mr. Slack, assessor from the Board of Guardians, who ran checks on those who had applied for financial assistance at the old workhouse on Eccles New Road. If help was granted,

it came in the form of vouchers for essential items. When the Jarrow Marchers passed through Pendleton, they were accommodated overnight at Brunswick Methodist Church, and a collection was made of both money and socks.

The people of Hanky Park formed a very close-knit community, and it was usual to hold 'open house' on occasions such as New Year. Greatly respected in the area were the volunteer workers, such as Mr. Greenhalgh, of the Barker Street Methodist Church, who created a homely and jolly atmosphere, and whose 'outings' are fondly remembered.

The Hippodrome in the 1940s

Ted Gray

The 'Salford Royal Hippodrome' was one of the theatres in the Percy Broadhead chain, and retained live stage shows long after the 'Palace' at the other end of Cross Lane had become a cinema.

In the years during and immediately after the Second World War, touring revues appeared with a different show weekly, performing twice nightly. Bottom of the advertising bills, but always first on the programme whilst the patrons settled in their seats, was an item regularly presented by a troupe of dancing girls, 'Millie Jackson's Young Ladies.' Their name would change slightly, depending on the title or theme of each week's revue. For example, if the revue was called 'French Follies' (very mild by today's standards), the girls would be billed as 'Millie Jackson's 8 Parisiennes,' or, if 'Arabian Nights' they would be 'Millie Jackson's 8 Ladies Of The Harem,' and so on. Even as regular patrons, it took us some time to penetrate the disguises offered by the various costumes and to realise that, although the main performers would move on to a different theatre (and different lodgings) each week, the dancers, probably for economy reasons, remained the same, and the eight ladies we were watching as 'Millie Jackson's 8 Lancashire Lassies' were the same individuals we had seen a week earlier as 'Millie Jackson's South Sea Islanders,' or whatever.

A comedian whose show was always full of goon-type humour (but long before the Goons became famous on radio) was Norman Caley, who was billed as 'The Mad Earl Of The Middle East.'

I saw him several times in the late-1940s, and my friends and I would try to remember his jokes and gags to try on unsuspecting school-mates who had not seen the show. We thought he was marvellous, but few people seem to have heard of him, and we never saw him in films or at more prestigious venues, and, presumably, he must have retired long before television came along.

A favourite whose annual appearance at the Salford Hippodrome was not to be missed, was Tod Slaughter. He and his company specialised in presenting melodramas such as 'Sweeney Todd,' 'Jack The Ripper,' 'The Ticket-Of-Leave Man,' and 'Maria Marten, or The Murder In The Red Barn.' Slaughter appealed to

SALFORD ROYAL **HIPPODROME**

CROSS LANE, SALFORD.   'Phone: PEN. 1065.
6-15   ::   TWICE NIGHTLY   ::   8-20

MONDAY, 10th JUNE, 1946, AND DURING THE WEEK:
Personal Appearance of the Stage, Screen and Radio Star,
TOD SLAUGHTER in the greatest of old time melodramas,

SWEENEY TODD

THE DEMON BARBER OF FLEET STREET

A full London cast including JENNY LYNN as "Mrs. Lovatt," of the Famous Pie Shop.
N.B.—Mr. Tod Slaughter hopes that the audience will be seated from the rise of the curtain at 6-15 and 8-20 as "Sweeney" starts to "polish 'em off" after the Overture, and continues his activities throughout this old London drama of the Demon Barber of Fleet Street. Tod advises you to book your seats early.

A 1946 newspaper advertisement for the visit of Tod Slaughter and his company in 'Sweeney Todd.' Note Tod's intention to "polish 'em off" promptly.

our teenage sense of humour, in that he did not take himself or his productions too seriously, and was quite happy to engage in banter with the audience. He could also be relied upon to introduce a novel note. For example, refreshments were not normally available at the Hippodrome, but during the run of 'Sweeney Todd,' Slaughter would arrange for meat pies to be sold in the interval, and his curtain speech (always to be relished as much as the play) would make reference to the finger nail found in Mrs.Lovatt's pie, and speculate as to the source of the filling in the Hippodrome pies. At the end of 'Jack The Ripper' he would remind the ladies that, although in the play they had seen Jack in the condemned cell, in real life he had never been found. With his sinister chuckle and leer, he would advise them to take care on the way home.

There is a story that during one performance by Slaughter, when he was on stage supposed to be looking for a victim who was hiding, a drunk in the audience shouted out, "He's behind the sofa." Slaughter paused, turned to the audience, and said, "Sir, I've been performing in this play for over thirty years, and I know he's behind the sofa!"

My friends and I attended Lees' Mission on Hodge Lane in the days when much entertainment was home-produced, and the 'Men's Effort' or 'Youth Fellowship Effort' would be a frequent Saturday evening fund-raising concert. We often arrived at the Salford Hippodrome armed with notebooks and pencils (especially if Norman Caley was on the bill) in order to steal any good ideas from the comic revues which we thought we might be able to copy in our amateur way for our next concert. On these occasions we would hope that the respectable ladies and gentlemen in the Mission audience had not been amongst patrons of previous 'efforts' at the Salford Hippodrome.

In its final years, the Hippodrome changed its name to the 'Windsor Theatre.' It was demolished in 1962.

The facade of the Salford Royal Hippodrome on Cross Lane, decorated for a Royal Visit.

Footnote: I had always assumed that 'Slaughter' was a stage-name chosen by the actor to match his image as the villain in so many melodramas. In checking some facts for this article, however, I was surprised to discover that Slaughter was, in fact, his real name and that only the 'Tod' had been invented. He was really N. Carter Slaughter, 1885-1956.

Hodge Lane Mission (Lees' Mission)

Marion Knowles (nee Thomas)

Hodge Lane Mission was an Independent Methodist establishment, founded by Mr. Lees, and so known locally as Lees' Mission. I remember attending Sunday morning services with my brother John, going home for lunch, then back again for Sunday School at 2.00pm. On Sunday evening, all the family attended the service. We children had to enter for Sunday School by the small door in Shah Street, the main door in Hodge Lane being reserved

The Boys' Brigade Band of Hodge Lane Mission, led by Harry Challinor, heads the procession in 1948 as it moves off down Lord Duncan Street. The two drummers, left and centre, are Ernie Short and Andrew Van Den Eden.

for the worshippers arriving for the main evening service.

There was always something going on at the Mission, and it was a centre for social life. Activities I recall include the Band of Hope, Junior Endeavour, Girls' Keep Fit classes (we all had blue dresses, and marched round the hall to the 'March of the Toreador'), choir, and so on. The Boys' Brigade always had a good time blowing bugles in Lord Duncan Street, disturbing my friend's lie-in on Sunday mornings.

On Saturdays there was usually a main event, planned well in advance, for which the organisers would prepare for many months. This could be the "Ladies' Weekend" or the "Men's Effort," on which occasions tea was served in the afternoon. To a child, it seemed one big party, with everything laid out on long tables, and everybody enjoying themselves. In the evening, according to whose weekend it was, there would often be a concert, and the same people would take responsibility for the evening service on the Sunday.

The young people played their part, too, and the "Youth Fellowship," organised by Frank Jones on his return from the forces, and other clubs, often produced fund-raising concerts, and an annual Christmas pantomime.

How we all managed to get ready, girls using the small room over the stage as a dressing room, with boys under the stage in the cellar, I will never know.

Another big occasion was Whit Sunday, with

everybody in their new clothes. Brother John would appear in his new suit, and I would have a new coat and hat, and everything that went with it. The major event of the day was the procession in the afternoon. This was an exclusive walk, reserved for Lees' Mission members only. The Mission did not join in the general Whit Monday walks. The Boys' Brigade band would line up first, at the top of Lord Duncan Street, all the members looking very smart, with instruments and leather belts shining, and their whites whiter than white. Next came the large banner, with Harold Jones and the other church elders and lay preachers, that is, those of them who were not doubling up by playing in the band. The ribbons on the banner were held by senior girls.

The small children came next, looking beautiful in their lovely dresses, and often carrying posies or baskets of flowers. Behind them came the junior children, and after them the seniors. Everyone looked really nice, and even the mothers treated themselves to new hats for the occasion. One year, my cousin May was a Rose Queen. She wore a lovely long dress, and carried a bouquet of flowers which had ribbons coming from it, which were held by her four attendants. I had the honour of holding the ribbon on one occasion. At various points in the procession, there would be smaller banners, made up of flowers, with messages such as 'God Is Love,' or 'Jesus Loves Little Children.' What a splash of colour!

Soon, the moment everyone had been waiting for would arrive. The Brigade band would start to play something like 'Onward Christian Soldiers,' and Harry Challinor, staff in hand, would lead off the procession. We would walk along Lord Duncan Street, turn into Cross Lane, and proceed to Unwin Square, where a short open-air service was held, the third Jones brother, Arthur, accompanying hymns on the portable harmonium. Then it was the walk back to the Mission. In the street outside, the band would play the 'General Salute' before dismissal, and we all went home for tea.

The annual Sunday School trip was another enjoyable event organised by the Mission. Greenfield was a popular venue. A good time was had by all, with games, races and a picnic. Then back home, tired and weary, but happy. In later life, we look back and realise how much we owe to those volunteer workers at the Mission.

Huddart St. Canteen (Free Breakfasts)
Bill Fereday

On cold, wet, windy mornings,
Outside Huddart Street canteen,
With a ticket of blue,
I would wait in the queue,
To hide shame, I'd try not to be seen.
The big boys would knee us and thump us,
(As if times were not tough enough)
But the pain I would feel,
Was being on a free meal,
Not being punched, and labelled a scruff.
Once inside, I would fill my tray quickly,
And sit on my own, near the back.
I would eat what I had in a hurry,
I was always ahead of the pack.
We were all in the same boat together,
Just Salford kids at that place in time.
I hope they all gained what they wanted in life,
And their dreams all came true – just like mine!

Irlams o' th' Height

Joyce Landers

For some years, I lived behind St.John's Church at Irlams O'Th'Height, and the memories I have of the shops along Bolton Road are as vivid as if they were yesterday. It was a favourite shopping area, very dear to local people.

Close to the traffic lights at the 'Britannia' public house, Mr. & Mrs. Binding had their sweet shop, always my first port of call when taking my son to school. Next came Blore's grocery store, where once each week the counter was loaded with bacon shanks to bring in the customers. Further along was Stott's greengrocery store. I was always told that to make a success in business, the shopkeeper must be friendly and cheerful in order to attract the clients, but the brothers who ran this shop proved this to be false. In the thirteen years I shopped there, I never remember a smile from either of them, but there was always a queue of people waiting to be served. Next door, the pet shop sold fresh meat until the outbreak of war. Then a Government ban came into force, and I remember the difficulty I had in persuading my spaniel to eat tinned dog food.

I was a regular visitor to the 'Bee Hive,' a tiny shop filled with wools of all the colours of the rainbow. Being a fanatical knitter, I spent many an hour selecting patterns and wool, and chatting with the owners. Not that I alone was to blame - my sons took long enough in choosing the colours they would like for themselves.

In Scholes' grocery store, a huge mound of New Zealand butter occupied a side counter, just waiting to be cut and patted into shape. I still claim that I have never tasted butter as nice as that from New Zealand. In this shop, the owners were very competitive with their prices, and so they were very popular with their clientele. Massey's was a family bakery business, and made bread and cakes which were hard to beat. Their display was always attractive, and it was hard to resist buying additional items, even if you had gone in only for a loaf.

Just past Tinkers, the chemist at Bank Lane corner, was Johnson's, where you could buy plump chickens and fresh fish, along with your greens. The last shop before Summerville Road was a children's delight, stocked with all the latest toys. The 'Dinky' cars I bought there must have cost me a small fortune, but how they lasted !

Returning from school in King Street, we walked home on the other side of Bolton Road, passing Ethel Reid's drapery store. Her son was Ken Reid, the famous cartoonist of the 'Manchester Evening News,' who created 'Fudge The Elf.' His books were real favourites with the children, and are probably collectors' items by now.

How many people recall the gift shop? It was full of items of jewellery and colourful knick-knacks to tempt the passer-by. I still have the watch my husband bought there long ago for my birthday, and it is still going strong. I also have a couple of brooches, which were presents on other occasions.

And then, Kidd's Fish and Chip Shop, well-known to Salford people, and widely held to be far better than Harry Ramsden's more famous establishment on the other side of the Pennines. When my sister came over from Canada, it was alleged that we nearly wore out the pavement between our house and Kidd's. Never a meat eater, she would head for the 'chippy' every lunchtime and suppertime that it opened, which, at that time, was daily. She couldn't get enough of Kidd's fried fish. When it was time for her to return, I remarked that she would miss Kidd's fish more than she would miss me. She even suggested that the Kidd family might consider opening a similar shop in Waterloo, Ontario!

Krinks, the hairdresser's shop, was nearby. Whenever I had a special occasion looming, few and far between until my children grew up, I would make an appointment there. Peter Krinks is still in business, but on Manchester Road, Swinton. I wonder whether he still supports Manchester City Football Club?

Alongside the hairdresser's was a sweets and tobacco shop owned by Mrs. Reid and her sister.

This always looked very dark inside, as it was a narrow shop with a long counter. There were a few round, black metal chairs, on which you could sit and enjoy a hot drink. My sons and I used to choose hot 'Vimto' on cold days after the walk from school.

I wonder how many men recall having their hair cut by Dickie Price, looking at the display of Rugby Football photographs which adorned the walls of his 'salon,' and listening to his opinions on the latest game.

Every week I would reach home laden with goods from shops on 'The Height.' I must have had strong arms in those days, but then so did most women. I cannot claim that I enjoy supermarket shopping, for all the choice it offers. The atmosphere, the gossip, and the personal touch is missing. But, this is another era. We can't turn back the clock, and I don't think I would want to, but I can still hold on to pleasant memories.

Bolton Road, Irlams O'Th'Height in the 1950s. Kidd's chip shop is in the centre of the row of shops on the left, a site now occupied by the 'Discount Giant' supermarket. Note the width of the road and the relative absence of traffic. The opening between the shops on the right led to Peter Andrew's coal yard. Nothing now remains of this scene.

A Jewish Childhood in Broughton

Dorothy Levy

I lived in Salford for 22 years, having been born in Kimberley Street in 1935. On my side of that street Jewish families alternated with Catholics, all living amicably together. (However, I do remember on one occasion being pursued by a boy who said, "You killed Jesus." I didn't understand what he was talking about.) At times of Passover and Jewish New Year my mother used to send a tray of Kosher Wine and Matzos, her home-made cakes, to our next-door neighbours. At Xmas we received in return a tray of mince pies, Xmas cake, sherry, and sweets.

I attended Marlborough Road School. As infants, each day we had to fold our arms across the desk and rest our heads upon them; sometimes we had a nap on camp-beds in the playground. For the Jewish children, Miss Slotki used to come once a week to teach Hebrew to the older children. At the outbreak of war in 1939, the whole school was evacuated to Pilling, near Fleetwood. We sat on a coach, all duly labelled, too young to understand what was going on. My label had the words "With Brother" added, whilst my brother, two years older than I, had "With Sister." This may have accounted for the fact that we were the last two children to be 'chosen' by foster parents from the Pilling Church Hall. The fact that we were the only Jewish children may have been the reason for the reluctance to accept us, although dietary considerations were abandoned for evacuees, so that was no problem.

Our foster mother, Mrs. Fishwick, was a kindly widow, with two teenage daughters. They lived on a small farm. We stayed for three years. Homesick at times, joyful when relatives came to visit, and sad on their departure.

Years later, my mother told me she had had a nervous breakdown at this time. No wonder, with three older sons in the forces, spread around the world, two youngest evacuated, and husband (my father) a reluctant Home Guard, still suffering from bouts of depression brought on by the effects of malaria contracted in the Middle East during the First World War.

We had occasional visits at the Pilling school from a Jewish couple, who chatted to us in a private room, and brought us sweets. Mrs. Fishwick would occasionally send a live hen to my mother – it would be put on the train at Fleetwood, collected in Manchester, and taken to be Kosher-killed, providing a welcome delicacy in the years of food-rationing. When I was older, I used to go to the Kosher Butcher, Sammy Shapiro, at the bottom of Bent Street, from where the myriad smells linger on. Bent Street had a brewery, a cigarette factory, and other assorted premises, all with fragrances of their own. The workers would often be cooling-off or lunching outside, and I hated having to walk past them.

At the age of 11 I attended Broughton High School. The Headmistress, Dr. Wicks, was a lovely lady, with a fondness for Scottish Country Dancing, which she taught. She was very understanding of the Jewish girls. Many of the orthodox followers

48

living nearby had to leave early on Fridays (before the Sabbath) and we all had Jewish holidays. Rabbi Caspar used to teach the Jewish girls once a week. My local library was at Mandley Park. It was an old building, with a musty smell - like the books, which were old and well-used. Bonfire Night was always a joint effort between Kimberley Street and Norton Street, the fire being positioned at the corner. On the following morning, each person was expected to remove a bucket of cinders to place in their own dustbin, so that the streets were soon clean again.

Broughton High School, attended by the writer, was on Bury New Road. The main school building was formed from the house 'Bella Vista'.

John Ridgeway

Minnie Adsley (neé Thorpe)

I first met John Ridgeway when as a child I attended St.Bartholomew's Regent Street Sunday School and the Children's Mission. Mr. Ridgeway was the Sunday School Superintendent. Years later I was a Sunday School teacher myself, also helping out at the Mission, and it was then that I came to appreciate what a great man Mr.Ridgeway was.

He was one of the sons of William Ridgeway, who had a scrap business in Essex Street, which ran parallel to Regent Street, both being off Oldfield Road, close to its junction with Regent Road. The other Ridgeway son was Alfred. John married Emily Hicks, and although they had no children of their own, they devoted their lives to the poor children of Salford.

John Ridgeway was a devout Christian, and during the First World War he had been a front-line soldier. His habit of kneeling down to say his prayers amused comrades in his billet, but when they realised how sincere he was, they came to respect him. After the war, he became a founder-member of the Old Salfordians' Rugby Club, and was the first club captain. His playing days ended in 1926, but he never severed his connection with the Club. He was also a long-time member of the Salford Lads' Club.

John and Emily bought a caravan at Bollington, near Bowdon, Altrincham, and the highlight of the Children's Mission calendar was the annual picnic, held in August. On these excursions, their caravan acted as kitchen for the whole company. Fortunately, the sun always seemed to shine for us on that day, and one of the farmers in the area used to allow us to pick fruit - an unusual and wonderful experience for a town child, and always a day to be remembered. Christmas was another time to be savoured at the Mission, and local firms were always prepared to provide gifts and assist in any way possible.

Sadly, those times have long since gone. The school has been demolished and the scrap yard has vanished. First, maisonettes were built on the site, only to be demolished in their turn, and now the new Sainsbury's Supermarket covers the whole area. John Ridgeway died on the 18th January 1959, aged 67. His wife Emily lived to be 90. Though I am now in my seventies, I will never forget the influence John Ridgeway had on the many children who lived in the Regent Road and Ordsall area of Salford.

Sunday School outing 1939; John Ridgeway standing at back.

stop, he threw over the controller handle too far and applied the emergency brake. The car stopped suddenly in its own length. We wondered what the passengers thought. The driver piloted the car over the large junction at Cross Lane, and then allowed John Morris to try the controls as far as Broad Street. In Frederick Road, my turn came, and I took number 361 down the hill to the stop near the depot.

Car number 350 was to be the official last tram. This tram had not been in service that day, but had been cleaned up specially for the occasion. It was waiting in the depot entrance, ready for members of the Transport Committee and other members of the Corporation. We were allowed on board to sit on the long seats in the lower saloon, and at about 10.10 p.m. we set off for the Docks. When we had crossed the junction at Cross Lane and were into Trafford Road it was realised that the last car from Manchester had still to arrive via Regent Road, so we were followed all the way to Ordsall Lane by this late-comer, which should have been in front. However, this 'rogue car' was reversed on the crossover facing Trafford Bridge and sent scuttling back to the depot.

At the Docks terminus we parked behind car 361, which had worked back from Frederick Road and was to precede the last tram. We waited a few minutes whilst photographs were taken, and then, at about 10.35 p.m., with the front window open and the car well-ventilated on that March night, we set off a few hundred yards behind number 361. The official party occupied the lower deck. The passengers on the top deck seemed indifferent to the occasion, and there was much noise and laughter. Crowds lined the route in places, as we swayed and hummed gracefully along Trafford Road and Cross Lane, like a ship at sea. Wheels groaned as we turned the corner into Broad Street, but then, as we gathered speed again along Frederick Road, we could hear the swish of the trolley-wheel

on the overhead wire as we coasted down the steep hill to arrive at the Depot gates. Here, most of the public disappeared into the night, but our group remained on the top deck and eventually we enjoyed the experience of being driven through the depot archway and into the shed. Here, a large number of staff and councillors had gathered, and we were told to come down. We obtained the driver's autograph, and more photographs were taken of the crew.

Then the General Manager, C.W.Baroth, made a speech, the main points of which were that the track was in a very bad condition, in parts positively dangerous, that the aged tramcars were now difficult and expensive to maintain, and that, despite the shortage of new buses, he had decided to discontinue the tram service. The Chairman of the Transport Committee also made a short speech, and with that little ceremony 46 years of electric tramway operation in Salford came to an end.

The last Salford tram to run in public service was on route 70 from the Docks terminus. Here it is, number 350, in drab wartime livery, seen in late 1946 in Ordsall Lane, just a few months before the end of tramway operation.

Life in Light Oaks Road, 1930

Dorothy Parkinson

Although I have lived on Light Oaks Road from the age of four in 1929, I can just remember a little of life in a small 'two-up-two-down' house off Lissadell Street, Broughton Road, Charlestown, where the front door opened from the living-room directly into the street. I don't know whether it was a very small room, but to me it seemed full of furniture, and there was an aspidistra on top of the sewing machine in the window, and nearby a caged bird. I would play either in the back-yard, or on the pavement outside the front door. Some people must have been extra house-proud, even to scrubbing the pavement, finishing off with varying shades of cream sandstone, or 'donkey stones.' Children had to be very careful not to stray on to a newly-cleaned frontage. The 'donkey-stones' were usually given by the 'rag-and-bone' man in exchange for old clothes.

When we moved, only a little over one mile away, we were almost on the edge of the old Salford, and there were farms and open fields beyond the bottom of our road towards Ellesmere Park, Eccles, and over to Swinton.

It seems incredible that where Light Oaks School is now, there was once a farmer's field, where as children we often played, making 'dens' out of the hay until we had to leave quickly when the farmer came along. Our road was one of three long roads, joining on to Lancaster Road, with a few intersecting roads. The houses were either terraced or semi-detached, with small gardens to the front and larger ones at the rear. I think the Heywood family were connected with building the houses on Light Oaks Road. All the houses are still looking good, though they must have been built 80 years ago. There were gates at each end of our road, and on Cholmondeley Road also. Several allotments were made available for the keener gardeners.

There were a few shops. Taylor's, the grocer-cum-everything shop, Alf Morrell's, the newsagents, and Miss Smith the draper. There was also the Eccles Co-Op butcher's and grocer's establishment on Hayfield Road, built in 1912, and now converted to flats. Coal was delivered by horse-and-cart, as was Jimmy Johnson's greengrocery. Milk was brought by a hand-cart, and ladled into jugs from a churn.

Lancaster Road finished at the bottom of our road in those days, but continued as a footpath through fields, past a Scout Hut, towards the golf course and Swinton. Along one section, the fences on both sides consisted of old iron and brass bedsteads, and was thus known as 'Bedstead Lane.' Other old names near to where the East Lancashire Road now runs, were 'Black Harry Bridge' and 'Squeeze Belly Entry.'

Swinton Fields were wonderful for children to play in, attracting mainly the boys, who used to collect frogspawn and tiddlers from the brooks and ponds, but I preferred to play on the sandhills, which covered the middle section of our road. We used to take picnics (bottles of water, with bread and jam) and spent many happy hours there. There was also Light Oaks Park, which has changed very little over the years. We were always wary at the approach of the 'Parky,' though I wonder why, as it never occurred to us to damage plants or property. In the park, the biggest change has been the demolition of the house and shop, and the provision of a children's play area. The groundsmen have to work much harder these days to keep the park looking so pleasant.

One of the highlights of the year for children was the bonfire which we had in the middle of our unpaved road. Parents were on hand to tend the fire, retrieve the potatoes when baked, provide the home-made treacle toffee, and generally help keep the occasion accident-free. My father usually had the job of making the 'Guy,' which was sometimes too life-like for me, and which I found rather frightening.

When I started school, it was at Broomhouse Lane (Hope), to where I walked with friends, and later with my brother, to and fro twice a day, and where we were shepherded safely across Eccles Old Road by our local 'bobby.' I loved this school, and the teachers we had, headed by Miss Westbrook. Classes, then called 'Standards,' 3 to 7 all shared the big hall, but this didn't seem to affect children's concentration. The 13-year-olds, Standard 7, were so few in number that they only just filled the back row of Standard 6, and they were taught by Miss Westbrook herself. Standards 1 and 2 were taught on the raised platform by Miss Robinson and Mrs. Cook. This part of the hall was partitioned-off after morning prayers. Miss Richardson taught Standards 3 and 4, and Miss Smith Standard 5. It being a Church of England school, we always had 'Scripture' (now Religious Education) for our first lesson, and once a week there was a service in Hope Church. A popular outing was to Seedley Baths for our swimming lesson, for which we walked both ways.

During the morning break, the older girls took turns at making coffee for the staff, using ground coffee, of course. Each teacher had her own cup, and one of the worst happenings of my school life was when I dropped all the crockery. I was petrified at telling the teachers what I had done, but fortunately they were very kind about the matter.

The East Lancashire Road was constructed in the early 1930s, and the building of houses and shops mushroomed so quickly that there were very few fields left by the start of the war in 1939. Our family moved, too, to where the sandhills had been, but the paving of the road had to wait until the end of the war. Until this was done, the surface was deeply rutted, and my father once witnessed a fire-engine coming down the road, followed by two of the firemen running behind, having been jolted off. Come to think of it, the road is not much better at the present time.

I'm glad to have experienced life when the roads were so much quieter.

Eccles Old Road, with Broomhouse Lane School on the left.

The Lodge Boy

Eddie Illston

Not many people will remember 'Lodge Boys,' but they were once an important part of the organisation of large factories. The 'Lodge' was at the entrance gate, and the gatekeeper was the receptionist and security guard of his day. He was assisted by a 'Lodge Boy.' I became the Lodge Boy at the Greengate factory of the Greengate and Irwell Rubber Company in 1935. In that particular firm, it was expected that a new recruit would hold the position for about six months before being appointed to a more responsible post within the Company.

In many respects, the Lodge Boys were glorified errand boys, but in a firm which expected value for money, they were also underpaid junior clerks. They were employed at the age of 14 and undertook a variety of work. The overall knowledge they gained of the various departments in a factory which produced such assorted items as electric cables, tennis shoes, leather shoes and slippers, fashion rainwear, and rubber-proofed fabrics, was invaluable.

At Greengate, the Lodge Boy's immediate boss was the Commissionaire, who was also responsible for the time-keeping and compilation of wages for about 600 employees. The Commissionaire was stationed at a high desk in the entrance Lodge, from which vantage point he could see through the windows and deal with any person wishing to enter or leave the factory. The Lodge Boy's place was in a cubby-hole under the stairs at the back of the Lodge. He shared this cramped space with a chest of drawers, which doubled as his desk, though there was no space for his knees, and sat on a small wooden stool, which had been knocked together in the engineers' workshop.

Overhead was an electric light bulb, and, further back, a water-sprinkler fire-precaution device. It was so dark that the electric light was kept on all day. The whole area was no more than four feet square. It was like a scene from Dickens.

A new Lodge Boy was allowed to learn his job under the supervision of the previous incumbent. All his duties were clearly outlined in a little black book, with the times at which they should be commenced and completed. His work began at 7.50 a.m., when he had to go round the factory unlocking the doors to various departments. At 8.19 a.m. the Commissionaire would switch on the electric bell which would ring outside the entrance to signal to the employees that they had one minute's grace before they would be locked out. At 8.20 he would switch off the bell and say, "Shut the gate, sonny." The Lodge Boy would shut the gate, but only after allowing one or two breathless sprinters to pass through.

All the employees, other than 'staff,' had a check-number. On arrival, the employee would unhook his metal disc from the checkboard and drop it into a box underneath. The Lodge Boy collected the checks, arranged them in numerical order, and then called out the numbers to the Commissionaire, who placed ticks against the names in the time-book. This Lodge Boy remembers particularly employee number 810, who always gave his check a polish on the seat of his trousers before dropping it into the box. It shone like burnished gold. The Lodge Boy would then replace the checks, about 400 in total, on the checkboards ready for the following day.

'Staff' members were treated differently. They were privileged. They did not have check numbers, but instead signed their names, with the time of arrival, on a sheet of foolscap paper. Officially, they started work at 8.30am, and, funnily enough, according to the time sheet, most people began work exactly on time. By 8.35am they were still signing 8.30, and it was not until about 8.40am that someone would finally capitulate and sign 8.31.

One of the Lodge Boy's tasks was to copy the times of arrival into the Staff Time Book, draw up a list of absentees, and then take the signature sheet and the absentee list to the Managing Director. When I did this, the Managing Director would suggest that I should come to work for him in the Clothing Warehouse. On each occasion, I thanked him politely, but refused his offer, saying that the Chief Clerk had promised that I could go into the General Office if I did well as a Lodge Boy. In fact, I was determined to succeed in this aim by making myself highly efficient at my job.

By the time the sheets had been delivered, it would be about 9.30am, and the Lodge Boy would take a cup and buy a pennyworth of milk from the grocer's shop down the street. On his return, he would make tea in the Commissionaire's jug. It was a strong brew - a dessertspoonful of 'Typhoo' tea, and three of sugar. I would help myself to one cup of tea, the rest being for the Commissionaire. The hot water was obtained from the 'steam kettle' in the yard, where a row of taps provided hot water for the brew-boys and girls who made the tea for the workers in various departments. There were no tea-pots – everyone used either mugs or jugs.

One day I was first at the steam kettle, and did not know that it had not been turned on earlier.

"My God, sonny, what have you done with that ?" said the Commissionaire, staring at the 'dead men' floating on top of the tea. I brewed some fresh tea, and made sure it never happened again.

In the afternoon, my duty included a tour of the garment-making departments to see whether anyone absent in the morning had come in for the afternoon. It was an embarrassing time for me, for I still wore short trousers. The girls would give wolf-whistles, and shout "Yoo, hoo," or "Look at his lovely knees." I would feel prickles all down my back as I hurried through the work-rooms. It was a great relief after three weeks when Mum finally raised enough money to buy a pair of long trousers.

In addition to the routine daily tasks, there were special jobs to do. On Mondays, the main job was stamping the employees' 'clock numbers' on the wage packets, which then had to be bundled for each department. Tuesday was 'Towel Day.' Hand towels were provided for the important members of staff, with roller-towels for the general workers. There were also a few unimportant young people on the staff who qualified for a hand towel - it seems that the final duty of a Lodge Boy before being promoted, was to add his own name to the list! About 120 Turkish hand-towels and 20 roller-towels had to be changed on Tuesdays. One oddity of this duty stemmed from the fact that the Chairman of the Board of Directors rarely used his towel. The Commissionaire decided that it was uneconomic to launder the hardly-used item, so instructed me to replace it, but to issue the almost-clean towel again to some unknown employee who would, unwittingly, share the Chairman's towel. However, I could not bring myself to give the used towel to anyone else. Fortunately, one fussy lady always wanted a nice, fluffy one, so I always placed the Chairman's fluffy and hardly-used amongst the ones offered for her choice. The bliss of ignorance - it never failed !

Wednesday was the last day of the 'working

week,' which left two days to make up the wages for Friday. The cutting room department had the very latest equipment - a time clock. So the Lodge Boy had to make out new cards and place them in their frames on Wednesday afternoon. Also, he had to wind-up the clock. I was quite small, so to reach the clock I had to borrow one of the cutters' stools to stand on. The clock's mechanism was stiff, and required quite an effort to wind it. I came in for some good-natured chaff from the cutters, but refused to allow anyone else to wind the clock for me. Wednesday was 'Pension Day' for the Commissionaire, who had 21 years' army service, and who wore the crown badge of a Regimental Sergeant-Major upon his arm. It was also his night out. He would arrive on the Thursday morning with a terrific hangover, so the Lodge Boy's first task was to collect a large bottle of lemonade from the local grocer. After his first long drink, the Commissionaire would smack his lips and groan, "That's better, sonny." But he didn't really recover until 11.30 a.m., after the Lodge Boy had been sent with the tea jug for a pint of Tetley's bitter from the 'Flying Horse.'

On one particular Thursday morning, I had a narrow escape when the jug was almost knocked out of my hand by the Chairman of the Board of Directors as he came through the swing doors. Fortunately, the Chairman was in a hurry and didn't seem to notice that the contents of the jug had froth on top. "That was a near one, sonny," gasped the Commissionaire.

Friday was 'Stamp Day.' Every employee had Health and Unemployment cards, which were kept in the Lodge. If the employee had worked all week, he had to make a contribution towards the cost of the stamps. This was done by sticking stamps on the cards, and deducting the contributions from the total wages. The Commissionaire had to visit the local Post Office to buy the stamps with a cheque made out by the firm's cashier. His brief absence gave the Lodge Boy a moment of glory. "Sit at the desk, sonny," he would say. "I won't be long." I would climb up on to the high chair and sit at the window ready to say, just as the Commissionaire did, " Now, Squire, what can I do for you ?" But Friday always seemed to be a quiet day, and nobody ever came.

Then came the stamp-sticking session, using a 'duck-pond,' a felt roller in an oblong dish of water. The Lodge Boy would be given the correct number of stamps for each department, and there would be quite a disturbance if he finished with one stamp over, or one stamp short. The error would usually be traced quickly, and by the end of the day, in addition to his normal daily duties, he would have stuck on over a thousand stamps.

Each year on Armistice Day, 11th November, at 11.00 a.m. the factory sirens and hooters would sound all over the city, and the bell would ring to signal the start of the two-minutes silence, strictly observed in memory of those who lost their lives in the First World War. On one such occasion, the Commissionaire stood at attention at his desk looking out of the window of the Lodge. I was not quite sure what to do, so I stood at attention in front of the chest of drawers. The Commissionaire said suddenly, "My God, sonny, look at that." He moved quickly out of the Lodge and across the street to where the Manager of the Clothing Machining Department was standing with his hat on his head. The Commissionaire's finger wagged. I couldn't hear what was said, but the Manager removed his hat like lightning. The Commissionaire returned to his post, breathing heavily for the remainder of the two minutes' silence.

After six months, the blow fell. "You'll be going to work in the warehouse a week on Monday, sonny," announced the Commissionaire. I stood there and my eyes began to fill with tears. "What's the matter, sonny ?" asked the Commissionaire. I could hardly speak, but managed to blurt out,

"When they sent me here from the Labour Exchange they told me it was for an Office Boy's job, then when I got here the Chief Clerk told me it was for a Lodge Boy's job, but that if I did well, I could go to work in the office."

"They can't do that to you, sonny," said the Commissionaire. "Not to the best Lodge Boy I've ever had." He put on his Commissionaire's cap and marched off to see the Company Secretary. When he came back, he said, "Don't worry about a thing, sonny. Leave it to me." Later in the day, the Commissionaire was called into the Company Secretary's office. He returned after a few minutes. "You'll be starting work in the office a week on Monday, sonny," he said.

The Commissionaire went and sat at his high desk and gazed out of the window. I sat at my chest of drawers looking across at the figure hunched over the desk, but, to me, it wasn't a bulky 50-year-old Commissionaire that I saw. History hadn't been my best subject at school, but I recognised a knight in shining armour when I saw one.

The Greengate area, as well as being the location of the Lodge Boy's factory, was also the site of one of the oldest buildings in Salford. This is the Bull's Head tavern, a medieval inn, reputed to be the oldest licensed house in England. It was closed in 1930 and demolished in 1937—38.

The Unknown Broughton Friend of L. S. Lowry

A talk given by Rev. Stanley Horrocks, summarised by Don Rainger

The main facts of the life of artist L.S.Lowry are well-known, but mystery surrounds his paintings of the lady known only as 'Ann.' Lowry was a very private person, and the friendship was kept secret to the end of his life. Would he have wanted the story told?

In the mid-1960s Stanley Horrocks visited the home of one of his parishioners from St. James' Church, Higher Broughton. He called this lady 'Miss Jones.' She mentioned that she had painted and sketched as a youngster, and she brought out a portfolio of 40 years' work, mainly drawings of old Salford, which she showed to the minister.

When she was ill in 1976, Miss Jones disclosed some of her earlier history. She had been born at 29 Wally Street, Higher Broughton, where her father had been a master painter and decorator. In 1910 the family had moved to 23 Teneriffe Street, and in 1913 to a corner shop at 27 Martha Street, near Phoebe Street, off Regent Road, Salford. By 1916 they had moved to 34 Gainsborough Street, where they stayed. Father died in 1934, and Miss Jones and her sister lived on together. Neither married.

Miss Jones had begun her education at Marlborough Road School, later moving to Salford Municipal Secondary School, situated behind the Chapel Street Education Offices. She matriculated in 1921 and went to work at the Steel Railway Metal Box Company at the corner of Frederick Road and Cheltenham Street. In 1922, when she was 17 and Lowry was 35, she became an art student at the Salford Royal Technical College, and here they met for the first time. Stanley Horrocks speculated that, as the friendship grew, Lowry may have travelled by train from Swinton, which he often did, to meet Miss Jones at Pendleton Station, from where they may have walked along Broad Street to the College.

Between 1924 and 1948 Lowry wrote 31 letters and 5 postcards to Miss Jones. The correspondence contained no close intimacy, and theirs was not a physical relationship. Miss Jones wrote to Lowry, but her letters to him have not survived. (Did Lowry's mother censor or destroy his mail?) During the time they were students, Lowry and Miss Jones went out on sketching trips together. She told Stanley Horrocks that they "walked out" for six years, sketching the same scenes together. She was fiercely independent, and resented any suggestion that she copied Lowry's style. Whereas he signed his work, she seldom did. It was she who urged Lowry to paint the now well-known self-portrait in 1925. He gave her a pencil sketch of himself, measuring some seven by six inches, which he'd had framed for her. He also presented her with a collection of Christina Rosetti poems.

Both Lowry and Miss Jones exhibited in Cheshire in 1926. The portraits Lowry painted of his parents have similarities to those Miss Jones painted of hers. Their landscape work showed they had similar styles, and it was clear that several street scenes had been painted from exactly the same viewpoints. Miss Jones never sold any of her pictures. Lowry thought that her best work was her antique drawings, but she destroyed all but three.

Miss Jones and Lowry last met in 1948, on Platform One of Victoria Station, when they went on an outing together. That was the year Lowry moved to live in Mottram. They never met or wrote to each other again. Lowry died on Monday, 23rd February 1976. Miss Jones died on a Monday in May 1977. Both were buried on the Friday following their deaths.

Why is their relationship of interest? Firstly, it goes some way to solving, perhaps, the mystery of 'Ann' in Lowry's life. But more importantly, it seems to have been Miss Jones who was Lowry's inspiration.

She it was who cared for him when he was ridiculed as a painter, and when he suffered terrible agonies in his private life. For that, art lovers must be grateful to Miss Jones. Her own portfolio survives, its location secret, but hope-fully in suitable conditions and being cared for as a remarkable complementary collection to Lowry's own.

There is a famous photograph, usually on permanent display at Peel Park, showing Lowry in an art class at the Salford Royal Technical College. He is seen standing at an easel. Four desks away, sits the bespectacled Miss Jones, hitherto unknown. Throughout their long friendship, and even when that photograph was mentioned in conversation, never once did Lowry indicate that he knew anyone in that class, let alone anything of their 25-year acquaintance. A very private man, Mr. Lowry. A most discreet lady, Miss Jones.

An art class in the mid-1920s at the Salford Royal Technical College shows Lowry, with hand on hip, standing at the easel right, whilst Miss Jones is at the third desk from the left.

Mark Addy, the Salford Hero

Tony Frankland

Mark Addy was born in April 1838 on the Manchester side of the River Irwell, near to Blackfriars Bridge, in the tenement known as the Stage Buildings. At this time, the river was widely used for recreation, and Mark's father made a living by hiring-out pleasure and racing craft.

Mark did not learn to swim until well into his

teens, but by the time of his death in 1890, he had saved well over 50 people from drowning in the river's murky waters. Whilst still a boy, he rescued a youngster by wading into the river up to his chin, and pulling the lad out. On a later occasion, he floated out on a plank to save another boy from drowning.

When he married, Mark moved into Salford and became the licensee of the 'Old Boathouse Inn' in Everard Street, off Ordsall Lane, close to the river. By this time he was a fine swimmer and oarsman, and whenever the shout went up that someone was in the river, Mark never failed to appear.

His bravery did not go unrewarded, for in January 1878 he was presented with a loyal address of appreciation and a purse of 200 guineas from the grateful citizens of Salford. He had already saved 37 lives, but continued to be on hand whenever help was required. For his courage, he also received the Silver and Gold Medals of the Humane Society for the Hundred of Salford, and the Bronze Medal of the Royal Humane Society. To this last medal, the members of the nearby Nemesis Rowing Club added a gold clasp as their personal token of appreciation. In June 1879 he was awarded the ultimate accolade of the Albert Medal, First Class. Mark headed a triumphant procession to the large assembly room in Salford Town Hall, where he was presented with the medal by Alderman Robinson, Mayor of Salford, on behalf of Queen Victoria.

On the evening of Whit Monday 1889, Mark,

now 51, made his final rescue. A boy had fallen into a badly-polluted part of the river, near to Factory Lane. Mark had to dive in three times before he successfully brought the boy safely to the bank, but in doing so he had swallowed a great deal of the filthy water. In a weakened state, he contracted tuberculosis and, after a long illness, died on the 9th June 1890.

On the 13th June he was buried in Weaste Cemetery, Salford, where a monument, paid for by public subscription, and unveiled by the Mayor, was erected to his memory. His portrait was placed in the Art Gallery at Peel Park, and a Memorial Fund of £100 was invested to provide prizes for swimming to Salford boys.

To this day, he remains a legend. The Everard Street footbridge is commonly known as Mark Addy Bridge, and in 1981 a new public house named 'The Mark Addy' opened on the bank of the River Irwell, near New Bailey Street Bridge, on the site of the old Nemesis Rowing Club. His monument may be seen in Weaste Cemetery.

Mark, Jim and Me – the birth of a pub

Wallace Brereton

In the 1970s and early 1980s, I was going around giving a lecture entitled 'The Irwell Saga.' There were no startling revelations in the narrative. Any patient researcher could glean the same details from library shelves. What made the talk unique were the many paintings, produced over several years, which I used to illustrate the events. In 1978 these pictures appeared in monochrome in a little book called 'The Irwell Gallery.'

This publication brought a steady stream of letters, covering topics ranging from school projects to general reminiscences. I thought that fame had arrived when one enquirer asked if he could use my paintings in a film report. Unfortunately, this turned out to be a very modest student effort. Then another writer told me he had purchased the old landing stage in Stanley Street, just by New Bailey Street bridge. I could be forgiven for being sceptical, for the former occupant (if you discount the rats) of this particular piece of river bank, had been the Nemesis Rowing Club in the earlier years of this century. But this latest enthusiast insisted that we meet that very night.

I protested that on that evening I intended to be present at a meeting of the Local History Society. "Where?" he asked. "Peel Park Library," I replied. He would not be put off. "Go a few minutes early, and we will talk outside." So, that evening I sat in my car outside the library, unsure what to expect. I did not have long to wait. A Rolls-Royce car drew up beside me, and the driver beckoned. It was my first meeting with Jim Ramsbottom.

Never before had I encountered anyone with such enthusiasm for the much-maligned River Irwell. I had always imagined that I was alone in my fascination for the river, but now, at last, there was someone else. Jim believed that the river could be a local asset, rather than a subject of civic shame. Whilst my ideas were in the realms of fantasy, he believed that he could actually effect a change. For over a hundred years, architects had turned the backs of their structures to the Irwell - Jim intended to build a public house boldly facing the waters. He envisaged the restoration of the old landing stage, and even talked of pleasure boats tying up there once again. The whole complex, he said, would be a shrine to the local hero Mark Addy.

I began to wonder whether Jim, too, was a fantasiser. At that time there were no pleasant riverside walks, with seats and trees, only grim Victorian warehouses and factories, many with unwashed windows, whilst here and there, small pipes discharged noxious effluent into the water. Despite his enthusiasm, Jim was a good listener, and devoured everything I had to say. He explained that every new pub needed a licence, and that was where I could help. There were so many pubs in the area, that any new one would have to be unique in some way, and Jim believed that when the application for a licence came before the court, a mature, staid person like myself), with some background historical knowledge, would impress the magistrates. The thought ran through my mind that here was an odd partnership - a rich young somebody, and a poor old nobody.

About a month later, on the day of the hearing, I met Jim in Bexley Square and together we went into the grim building. The licence was granted without any fuss. I was not called to speak in support, but I like to think that my written report had been of some use. In theory, the building could now go ahead, but many months were to elapse before there were any signs of activity. The Irwell had to wait for its transformation.

A few days after our first meeting, we had met again in a small bar in Bridge Street, this time in company of Brian Green, of the Inland Waterways Association. As a result, Jim and Jean Ramsbottom, my wife Margery and I, found ourselves treated as honoured guests in the Lord Mayor's parade of boats on the occasion of the Inland Waterways Association rally. Seated in the prow of a narrowboat, we were able to view the site of the proposed pub. It was still untouched, but a colourful orchestra was on the spot, playing a

Wallace Brereton's drawing of 'The Mark Addy' from the river.

lively tune. The date of that pleasant interlude was Saturday, the 25th August 1979. The organisers of the rally gave me a brass plaque to screw to the bulkhead of my boat - if only I had one!

Work on site started in 1980, and I was pleased to be kept informed of progress. The problems would have deterred a lesser person than Jim Ramsbottom. Whilst the foundations were being prepared, unexpected streams of water appeared from several sources. I was aware that there had been a spring about a hundred yards downstream, which had once fed a spa bath. Perhaps modern building technology had disturbed the surroundings. Whatever the reason, the difficulties caused work to cease for about six months whilst the source of the seepage was traced, and at one time it was extremely doubtful whether there would ever be a 'Mark Addy' pub. But Jim's ability to laugh in the face of adversity proved an admirable quality.

Work eventually recommenced, and passers-by on Albert Bridge saw a strange framework begin to grow on that small foothold of grass beneath Stanley Street. It must have been rather a precarious site for the workmen, but I did not hear of any serious mishaps. When the outside shell of the building had been completed, Jim collected Margery and I in the Rolls and we went along to examine progress. We stood chatting amongst the hammering and sawing of the craftsmen. There had been heavy rain the day before, and all kinds of rubbish was floating down the river, in addition to the usual oily slicks. As one who had taken an interest in the Irwell for so long, I felt strangely, though unreasonably, responsible for its condition. I almost apologised, but instead said, "It's a pity that the customers will have to see all that." The ever-optimistic Jim brushed this objection aside. "On the contrary," he said, "they will find it all interesting - look, there goes an old fridge door."

On the day of the grand opening ceremony in 1981, Margery and I were just two of the many guests who enjoyed a magnificent buffet. Now, 'The Mark Addy' is well-established as one of Salford's favourite rendezvous. On the wall inside hangs one of my paintings, my remaining link with the enterprise. Jim Ramsbottom has moved on to other, larger and more ambitious developments, each, no doubt, with its own agonies and ecstasies, but I would wager (odds-on) that 'The Mark Addy' has a special place in his affections.

At the end of Stanley Street, managers of the Castlefield Heritage project have erected a sign giving information about the New Bayley Prison and the old landing stage. It bears an illustration of a Packet Boat that has obviously been copied from my painting. When I researched these passenger boats, I was unable to find any pictures in the archives, and so the boat on my painting in 'The Mark Addy' is pure conjecture. The boat on the sign has been given an extra sail - it would seem that the person responsible has mistaken a shadow on my picture! There is no reference or acknowledgement of the source of the drawing, but I, like Jim, can laugh in the face of adversity ...

Wallace Brereton and Jim Ramsbottom at the opening in 1981.

Memories

————————— Margery Brereton

Where has Regent Road gone?
Long time a-finding
Where have all the shops gone?
What is now abiding?

Where has Ordsall Lane gone?
With tenements arising
The clanging trams have gone
New flats are uninspiring.

Where has Cross Lane market gone?
With cattle there for sale
The Picture House and Theatre gone,
Or is my memory stale?

Where have all the people gone?
High-rise flats, all of them
Where have all the workmen gone?
To take those flats down again.

Where has the charm of childhood gone?
My school, and the tripe works?
The safe walk to Peel Park gone,
Where no danger lurked.

Where have all those places gone?
Was it magic, as it seems?
Have all those far-off days gone,
Or was it in my dreams?

*A 'knocker-up,' as remembered by Miriam Wells, at work
tapping on upstairs windows to waken the occupants. This
particular man carried on his rounds even as late as the
1950s.*

'Milk – Oh'

Ken Heys

As a boy, I lived in Hyde (where they say flies go in the winter time), on the Cheshire side of Manchester, but Grandfather lived in Clifton, on the Lancashire side, and that was where I chose to spend most of my school holidays. The house, opposite St. Anne's Church Sunday School, was next door to the Seven Stars Farm, owned by the brothers Frank, Harry, and Tom Fish.

Grandad must have retired about 1935. He once took me to his factory at Moses Gate, Farnworth, which was rather derelict and contained thousands of rusty steel hoops, which had been intended to hold cotton bales togther. I learnt later that during the depression of the 1930s, the cotton market had slumped, and Grandad's stock of hoops became worthless and led to his bankruptcy. Nevertheless, he remained a jovial man. I remember him as bald-headed, bespectacled, and well-built, with a moustache which he would wax and twirl. His shirt-sleeves were always rolled-up above the elbows, and he regularly wore a waistcoat, across which he fastened his watch chain. He always had a twinkle in his eye, and despite his size, he was a most gentle person. Up at the crack of dawn, he would breakfast on porridge and honey, the latter bought from Lewis's in Manchester in 6lb. drums, and then dig in the kitchen garden, encouraging me to do the same. During the 1939-45 War he was a great supporter of the 'Dig For Victory' campaign to encourge home-production of vegetables, and his crops kept us well-supplied.

Grandad became the odd-job-man for the Fish Brothers, and he could often be found on their farm fixing anything from wagon-wheels and gates, to washers on taps. Farm tools presented no problem to him, and many a time he refused payment for jobs, saying he enjoyed being of use in his old age.

My favourite jobs on the farm were 'mucking-out' the cow-sheds and horse stables, feeding the animals, and grooming 'Dobbin' ready for the daily milk round. I loved to harness the horse and lead him across the cobbled yard to the water-trough. When he had quenched his thirst, I would help secure him in the shafts of one of the milk carts. One cart had a canopy, which offered some protection for

Farmer Charlie Cawthorne of Green's Farm, Clifton

the driver in wet weather, and there was sometimes some competition for the use of this one. Bringing the cows to their stalls was another job. Later, I was taught how to milk, but my small hands were no match for the large fingers of the Fish brothers. Tom Fish would enjoy the occasional prank, and from the next stall would squirt milk down my neck. It was some time before I mastered the art of directing the milk into the bucket.

A large gate separated the 'pond' field from the farm yard. From Grandad's house, we could always tell when it was milking time, because the cows would come from far away across Clifton Moss and gather by that gate. Their timing was impeccable!

At harvest time, extra helpers would be recruited for hay-making, and work would continue until it was almost too dark to see the way home. The bales would be stacked to a great height in the enormous barn. Children loved to play hide-and-seek, or build dens, in the barn, much to the farmer's annoyance if he caught them.

The dairy opened early, and the large milk churns were loaded onto the milk carts. Essential equipment included the ladles for measuring half-pints and pints. The round with which I was most familiar took us towards Kearsley and Unity Brook as far as Moss Lane Post Office, returning via Dixon Fold to St.Anne's Vicarage and the Alms Houses on Manchester Road. I was always amused by the customers who placed their milk jugs outside,

A milk float, similar to the one described by the writer. This one belonged to Leonard Potter of Ivy Farm, Pendlebury, not far from the Clifton Farm described in the article.

with either a slate or a tile on top to keep the dust and the cats out. Sometimes a customer would complain of short-measure. Then Frank would pour the milk from the jug back into the measure to prove his point. The round finished after 11.00 a.m. near Woodgate Row. I felt sorry for the people who had to live there. It was below street level, and the downstairs windows looked out on to a brick wall only three or four feet away. Anyone walking along the main road could look through the railings into the bedroom windows.

I earned my first wages in the week before my 13th birthday. It was wartime, Dad was away in the army, and as I had helped for six years without pay, I decided to ask Frank for some wages. After some humming and hawing, he agreed to pay me thirteen shillings and fourpence per week. On receiving my first payment, I checked it and found that it amounted to only thirteen shillings. With some trepidation, I approached Frank and asked him to count it. "Well, that's right, isn't it?" he said. "I only said thirteen bob." I stuck my ground and said that if he didn't pay me the extra fourpence

I would never work for him again. He laughed, but saw I was serious when I threatened to go for Grandad to sort him out. He laughed again, but paid the missing fourpence. This became my regular holiday wage for the next four years – no increments, so Frank won in the long run.

Milking by hand soon gave way to electrically-powered machinery, and the metal measures were replaced by more hygienic bottles with cardboard tops. 'Dobbin' and the milk carts, too, were destined to be substituted by mechanised transport. Happy days long gone, when a pint of milk was only fourpence (old pennies, at that), and the delivery men could enjoy the wit and chat of the customers. I loved to listen to my Grandad, who could remember when the milk was only a half-penny per pint at the corner shop. My reminiscences hardly compare with his, but all memories are precious! Nowadays, who could guess that there was once a farm on the site of the Chloride Recreation Club, or the Seven Stars Coaching Inn facing St. Anne's Church? And who would have guessed that it would become part of Salford?

Manchester Road, Clifton, near Pendlebury, was the centre of Ken Hey's boyhood milkround. The view is looking towards Bolton, with St. Anne's Church roof visible centre right.

The Office of the Salford Royal Technical College, 1945–1965

Joyce Wolfendale and Marion Ward

We were fortunate to work in the College office during one of the most interesting times in its development. The College dated from 1896, when it had been officially opened by the then Duke and Duchess of York. Today it is that part of Salford University known as the Peel Building. It was refurbished and re-opened in 1987 by the present Duchess of York.

In 1945, when I first went to work there (Marion joined me in 1953), the College office was on the left of the main entrance. It was a large, square room, with a solid wooden counter, which had heavy drawers and cupboards underneath. The drawers had brass handles. There was also a cast-iron fireplace with a real coal fire, which had to be kept fuelled from buckets of coal brought in by the porters. Part of the office was sectioned-off to make a private portion for the Registrar, and this was fitted with wooden panels with stained glass windows at the top. The pedestal telephone was housed in a kind of 'phone box, and there were only two or three extensions for the whole of the building.

In the middle of the room were sloping desks, made to hold very large ledgers, with ink-wells at the top. One of my first jobs was to make the post stamp book balance, and I couldn't do it and went home in tears. Later, I realised that post books never seem to balance, anyway.

The three typewriters were either pre-war or army surplus, and did not make life easy. Many years later, we thought the first electric typewriters, which returned the carriage automatically, were wonderful. Teaching staff had to write most of their own letters, and on one occasion, as an office junior was carrying the mail to the Post Office near the corner of Cross Lane and Broad Street, a gust of wind blew most of the letters into the canal as she was crossing Windsor Bridge. An obliging porter fished them out the next day, for the density of the water meant that most were floating, and the staff concerned gallantly re-wrote their correspondence.

Behind the College was a house which once had been the residence of Peel Park's Head Gardener. Here were stored old office records and uncollected certificates, some of which dated back to the early 1900s, and were large and magnificent. There were heavy metal boxes, with student record cards in them, all hand-written in copperplate. Nothing was ever thrown away. Even though these items were very dusty, it was always interesting to have to search for a particular record. Most old records requested were from unsuccessful students - which made us wonder. Later on, the School of Chiropody was housed in this building before it was moved to 28/29 The Crescent.

A pre-fabricated canteen, which is still there, was built in front of the house. Students used to hold 'tea dances' there from about 4.30 to 6.00 p.m. before evening classes, and these were great social events. The canteen was also used during the evenings in the Summer by the office staff to write-up all the student records for the next enrolment in September, and to send out results to students. This work was copied by hand, using pen and ink, from large sheets of results sent in by the teachers. The first ball-point pen I ever saw was owned by the Head of the Chemistry Department, and was thought to be a great possession.

In 1945 there were few full-time students. Others were on day-release from their jobs, but most were evening-class pupils. Classes were held every evening until 9.30 or 10.00 p.m., and also on Saturday mornings. Many students would attend for three evenings per week, plus Saturday, after having worked full-time all week. Later on, 'Sandwich Courses' were introduced in co-operation with local firms, some of the programmes being tailored to the requirments of companies such as Metropolitan Vickers of Trafford Park, or Gardner's of Patricroft. The first 'Sandwich Courses' lasted four years, each having six months full-time in College and six months in industry.

Dr. Venables, the Principal during the late-1940s and early '50s, was a man of vision. He believed that technical education was a 'retriever,' or a safety net, for those who perhaps had not succeeded

Technical College, Peel Park, Salford

The impressive building of the Royal Technical College in Peel Park was opened in 1896 by the Duke and Duchess of York as the 'Salford Technical Institute.'

in other forms of education. The day to ask him for a rise was the day he heard that someone who had left school at the age of 14 had, through the resources of the 'Tech,' gained a Ph.D.

From 1948, the College grew rapidly. Teaching staff increased in number. Telephone facilities were improved to give three outside lines and twenty extensions, and a switchboard was installed. This had plugs, winking eyes, and crossed wires, and made people very angry. The growth in numbers of students meant that the emphasis moved gradually from evening classes to day-release and 'sandwich' courses. The Principal grabbed as much advanced work as he could (permission to run advanced courses had to be gained from the North-West Regional Academic Committee), and gradually the College became an institution where all types of technical education, from sheet metal working and terrazzo tiling to courses of University standard, were available. But this proved unwieldy, and the College was split into the College of Advanced Technology (now Salford University) and Peel Park College (later Salford Technical College, then the Salford College of Technology, and now itself split into University College of Salford and Salford College of Further Education).

During the 1950s there was an acute shortage of accommodation, and classes were held in most unsuitable places, including corridors and the canteen. At one stage, there were outbuildings all over the city - a former chapel in Woodbine Street (one terraced house bought and another just 'acquired' by the teaching staff); the Sons of Temperance building at 40 The Crescent (where staff and students worked in coats in winter) ; and Brunswick Chapel (where there was a mouse problem). One year, students queried the room allocated for their class. It was a toilet and, knowing the desperate situation, the students thought it might be correct - it wasn't.

Each Spring, the College took over the Art Gallery at Peel Park and two rooms were set up for examination candidates. Up to 150 students, taking assorted subjects, could be accommodated, with one invigilator for every 30-40 candidates. In one of the galleries, the absence of a clock was rectified by hanging a timepiece on a string round the neck of the marble statue, 'The Genius Of Lancahire.' One wonders what inspiration the students gained from this. Great use was made of Peel Park Library, as the College had no library of its own until 1958.

We can recall two fires - one in the electrical switchboard, which was housed in the stationery office, and which put all the telephones out of action. Someone had to run across to the Fire Station to raise the alarm. Another fire was in the sub-station in the basement corridor. When this blew, it affected a wide area, and the telephones to the Electricity Board were jammed - we had to ask the operator to relay the information as to the source of the trouble.

The main hall (Peel Hall) with its steeply-raked seating and magnificent pipe-organ, was used for assemblies, music concerts, and meetings. At Christmas, the student concert sometimes got out of hand and had to be stopped by the Principal. The organ was later transferred to the University's Maxwell Hall, but when we were young we were sometimes invited to see the organ loft. We regarded this as just a bit of fun - nowadays it would be called sexual harassment.

Important visitors were vital for the growth and recognition of the College. For these occasions, a silver service was provided for lunches in the Committee Room, there being no suitable dining area. We were privileged to be present when the Queen opened the University Buildings, and when the Duke of Edinburgh opened the Salford College at Frederck Road, both of us having been involved in the preparations for these ceremonies. We both continued to work in education until we retired, but never was it so much fun as when the College was fighting to climb the ladder on a shoestring budget.

The 'Open Air' School at Swinton

Jean Gilliland

In 1918 an Open-Air School experiment with a class of what was then termed "physically defective children" was begun in, of all places, the bandstand of Victoria Park, Swinton. This experiment had a more far-reaching effect than could have been visualised at the time. By the September of that year, severe weather had made it impossible to continue conducting a school in the bandstand, and the children were moved into the Swinton Cricket Club pavilion in Milner Street (now demolished). Later, two army huts were converted, and became the site of a successful Open Air School under the direction of Miss Brobson, the Headmistress.

By the mid-1930s the Swinton & Pendlebury Education Committee had decided that a more suitable building was required. Mr. Hubert Bennett, A.R.I.B.A., designed a new school costing £11,000. It offered accommodation for 135 scholars, and was intended to provide education for children

"Rest" at the Open Air School, 1934.

between the ages of three and fourteen years. It was opened on Barton Road on the 17th May 1938. An article in 'The Journal' explained its function:"The Open-Air School was not merely a school in the open air; it combined a way of life and a system of treatment which included seven special features.

1. Fresh air and sunlight.
2. Proper diet.
3. Rest.
4. The hygienic way of life.
5. Individual treatment.
6. Medical treatment.
7. Special educational methods.Fresh air and sunlight were Dame Nature's finest tonics, and the much-abused English climate had bred a vigorous and hardy race."

Transport was provided for the children by the Lancashire United Transport Company, which charged £1 per day for two vehicles.

In September 1977 Alfred Morris, then Minister for the Disabled, opened the extension which had been made to 'Parkfield,' the former 'Open Air School.' The Minister commented on the new facilities now available and congratulated everyone involved in planning and working the new areas.

By 1983 the number of children attending Parkfield had declined sharply, as also had the number on roll at Oaklands School, Broughton. It was decided to amalgamate the two schools, retaining the centrally-situated Parkfield site. The new school was called 'Parklands' and provided education for pupils from 3 to 18 years of age. However, numbers continued to decline steadily, and in 1991 'Parklands' became 'Parkes Field.' The buildings on Barton Road now contain two separate units.One is Parkes Field Primary School; the other houses Salford Education Department's Support Service.

What will these buildings be in the year 2018? Still used for education, or abandoned and demolished?

Washing time at the Open Air School, 1934.

Parks of Salford Remembered

Don Lingard

I was fortunate as a child to live only a stone's throw from Seedley Park, which in the 1930s was separated from Buile Hill Park by railings and a gate which was locked at night. My first recollections of the parks include distant memories of being taken by my mother, pushing the pram containing my baby sister, to picnic on the well-kept lawns opposite the Museum. In those days, the restaurant adjoined the Museum, and it was possible to purchase hot water with which to make your own tea. It seemed that many young families took advantage of this facility, and they could be seen spreading their tablecloths and enjoying afternoon tea on the grass.

Another favourite pastime in the summer was to sit and watch games in progress on the bowling greens in Seedley Park. On big match days you had to arrive early in order to get a seat. On one occasion, accompanied by my mother, I tried to ride my tricycle down the steps which led to the Greens. I survived without serious injury, but remember having a drink from the ornamental fountain which was situated in the middle of the main walk. Years later, I learned to play bowls on the Ladies' Green, which doubled as the Learners' Green.

The duck pond in Seedley Park boasted many species of ducks and swans, but 'our gang' was mainly interested in the tiddlers, goldfish, and tadpoles. Every summer, armed with new fishing nets and jam jars, we would climb over the railings, quickly bag a few fish, and be away before the Park Keeper could catch us.

Even to my childish eyes, both Buile Hill and Seedley Parks had beautifully-manicured lawns and well-kept flower beds, plus an abundance of shrubs and giant trees of every variety. Although there were numerous uniformed park keepers with whistles and sticks, plus gardeners, keeping everyone and everything in order, and whilst there were many 'Keep Off The Grass' signs, there was still plenty of space to play and explore. The swings and roundabouts were favourites with the children, but, in addition, there were the tennis courts (where everyone played in white), a putting green, a pitch

The mansion in Buile Hill Park was built by Sir Charles Barry in the 1820s. It was converted into a Natural History Museum in 1906, and is now the Mining Museum.

and putt course, bowls, and, of course, the Museum.

What is now the Mining Museum, was then a Museum of Natural History. That was the place to visit on a Sunday afternoon, because, when dressed in your best clothes, the attendant would usually let you in through the turnstile - that is, if you appeared to be well-behaved. The Museum contained a magnificent collection of stuffed animals, including two ferocious lions fighting, and a display of skeletons of the upper primates, all particularly fascinating for young children. In glass cases were housed collections of fossils and minerals, and as one grew older, more was learned about the museum exhibits.

During the 1939-45 War, the Park changed. The cafe adjoining the Museum had already been demolished, a new one having been built on the site of the old grass tennis courts. Personnel of the Royal Air Force appeared to man a barrage balloon site in front of the Museum, and in Seedley Park trench air raid shelters were built. The duck pond was filled in, and the railings enclosing the park were taken away to be melted down as scrap metal to help the war effort. A general air of neglect seemed to settle over the whole place.

However, after the war, even though austerity was the order of the day, the Park revived. Brass bands played once again in the old bandstand (the new bandstand near the tennis courts had been dismantled), and the new cafe seemed quite 'posh,' for here you could be served with afternoon tea by a Head Waiter in full dress, or by a waitress smartly attired in traditional black-and-white outfit. In the early 1950s, the atmosphere in the cafe altered slightly, and it became less sedate with the influx of young people.

Most of my memories of Buile Hill are of summer months in the 1930s and 1950s, when, on Sunday afternoons in particular, it seemed that hundreds of people thronged the park, strolling round its many paths, and lingering in the then beautiful conservatory to admire the tropical plants and fishpond. And not a vandal in sight!

Twelve months before the outbreak of the 1939 war, my family moved to a house on the other side of Langworthy Road, and although I still kept my old friends, I became acquainted with Langworthy Park, known usually as 'Chimney Pot Park' on account of its high level, or 'Reservoir Park,' from its origin as a reservoir of a Manchester and Salford Water Company. It consisted mainly of two very good bowling greens, a couple of plots of grass for play purposes, some flower beds, and a recreation ground. It was a nice little place, in a built-up area. During the war, the walls, ten feet thick, were drilled into, and a large air raid shelter was constructed under the park. Sadly, bomb damage caused much devastation to 'Chimney Pot Park.'

My introduction to Peel Park came via my grandfather, again in the 1930s. We had walked through Wallness, which to me seemed quite rural, and standing on the top of the terrace at the rear of the Art Gallery, we had a grand view looking down the majestic flight of steps to a beautiful floral display and the

Peel Park Terrace, behind the Art Gallery, and the cannons mentioned by the writer.

bandstand, as seen in Lowry's paintings. On a clear day, it was possible to see for miles, and various landmarks were pointed out to me, including the old windmill on the other side of the Irwell, just beyond the 'Meadow.' On the terrace itself, were two big cannons and a fenced-off pile of cannon balls. I was told that they had been captured at Sebastopol during the Crimean War. Alas, they, too, were taken away for the 'War Effort!'

Peel Park was said to be the first public park in Salford, and had, and still has, a fine Art Gallery, Museum, and Library. The latter was the first unconditionally free public library in the United Kingdom. Of the assorted treasures in the Museum, I remember best the large golden figure of Buddha which stood at the head of the staircase.

Two incidents concerning Peel Park remain in my mind - firstly, the great flood of 1946, and, secondly, the filming of "Hobson's Choice."* I used to cycle from my home near the Castle Irwell Racecourse through the park on my way to work at Dorman & Smith, and on the morning of the flood noticed that the water level in the river was very high, but thought no more about it. But on my return from work at about 5.15 p.m., the sight of Peel Park was astonishing. The lower portion was flooded to a depth of several feet, the water almost reaching the top of the bandstand, and buildings by the bowling greens and tennis courts were practically submerged. It was a sight never to be forgotten.

That excellent play and film "Hobson's Choice" helped put Salford on the map, and the producer's decision to film some scenes in Salford was inspired. I watched from a distance the scene where Will Mossop (played by John Mills) courts Maggie Hobson (Brenda de Banzie) on the river bank. A dummy gas lamp and bench seat were provided opposite the Adelphi, where the film crew had to introduce foam onto the river to make it look more authentic.

From the terrace, a steep flight of steps led to the lower portion of Peel Park, which was subject to flooding.

Peel Park had all the usual amenities in the way of bowling greens, tennis courts, children's playground, etc., but never quite gained the prestige of Buile Hill. At one time, a great deal of tipping took place, especially on the David Lewis Recreation Ground. Fortunately, it now seems to be recovering, and if the Irwell can be cleaned up even more, and if the University makes no more encroachments, the park may well become the envy of many cities.

Set in the prosperous part of Pendleton was Light Oaks Park, which I visited only rarely. Although fairly small, it was, and still is, splendidly laid-out. The better-off residents of Salford frequented this park, and its tennis club was quite exclusive.

Albert Park, Lower Broughton, was the last of the Salford parks I knew. It used to have a nice formal layout, with pretty flower beds set either side of a long central walk, lined with classical statues. It, too, had bowling greens, tennis courts, and a splendid lake. Now, alas, there are only football pitches.

*(Footnote: * Hobson's Choice (the novel) £4·95 — see back of cover)*

Pendleton and Pigeons

Bill Lynch

In our two-bedroomed house in Florin Street there were eight of us, Mum, Dad, and six children, of whom I, born in 1913, was the oldest. As the 'senior,' it fell to me to help look after the others, especially when there was any illness, and, consequently, running battles with the truancy officer, the 'School Board,' were not unusual. When I was about ten years of age, we must have 'come into money,' for suddenly our home suffered an upheaval. Out went the old gas mantles, and in came new electric lights. Four lights and one power socket, all for two pounds ten shillings. It was fascinating to be able to touch a switch and find the room flooded with light. In the first few days, we must have added mightily to our bill just by compulsively switching the lights on and off.

I used to earn pocket money by delivering coal, obtained from the local coal yard, to people in nearby streets. I also chopped wood and made bundles of fire-lighters. Later, I sold newspapers for a shop in High Street run by Bill Southwood. On Fridays I would go round Broad Street and Whit Lane with copies of the 'Salford Reporter.' On Saturdays between 1.00pm and 6.00pm I sold racing papers. These were printed every hour, but the last edition was the most fought over, for this carried all the results for the full day. With this I used to run through all the streets off Ellor Street, and then into Seedley.

Leaving school at the age of 14, my first real job was at Larmouth & Bulmer's engineering firm in Unwin Square, brewing-up for the skilled men. In time, I became a centre-lathe turner, and although the basic training was good, in later life I realised that the methods were crude. The machines, which were driven from a line shaft, were illuminated by gas lights, and suspended from a rail above each lathe was an old tin can, with a hole punched in the bottom, which allowed an oil-and-water liquid called 'Mystic' to drip on to, and cool, the cutting tools.

Pigeon-fancying took my interest, as many youngsters kept birds in their back-yards. A pigeon could cost anything from sixpence to five shillings. Often we would buy from other owners in the neighbourhood, but then we took the risk that the bird would fly back to its original home before it had been re-trained. We made sure that the bird returned only to its home loft by pairing a cock with a hen, so that, when released, the cock would speed back to reach its hen. I joined the Pendleton Homing Society about 1927. There were other similar clubs all over the city. Some short-distance races were arranged, these being over distances about a mile, but the Homing Races involved crating the birds and sending them for release from some distant railway station. On Friday evenings, the rubber rings and sealed numbers were attached to the birds' feet, and then on Saturday the release would be timed so that the birds would not reach home before about 2.00pm, as we all worked Saturday mornings. Small bets added to the excitement, and each weekend the pigeon races must have brought pleasure to many Salfordians.

Pendleton Co-operative Industrial Society

———— Mrs. Ida McClenahan remembers.

(Additional material from a booklet loaned by Mrs. Dorothy Parkinson)

In 1910 the Pendleton Co-Operative Industrial Society celebrated its 50th anniversary. From small beginnings in 1860 in a single shop at 155 Broad Street, it had grown into a mighty business, with numerous branches, which, in one form or another, catered for every need. It was said that the Co-Op could look after you from the cradle to the grave.

The increase in the number of its branches, together with the fact that the Eccles Society had opened a branch at Irlams O' Th' Height, led to negotiations with neighbouring societies to define boundaries. As a result, the arrangement with the Manchester & Salford Co-Op saw a demarcation at Windsor Bridge, where the Pendleton Society agreed to have branches on the right-hand side of Cross Lane only. The Eccles Society agreed to encroach no further on the Pendleton district. All societies were afiliated to the Co-operative Wholesale Society (CWS), an organisation set up to purchase, produce, and distribute goods to the shops – a universal provider. This was followed by its own bank, insurance company, printing works, and factories producing foodstuffs, clothing, furniture, etc. The biscuit works at Crumpsall was known for its 'Crumpsall Crackers,' and it was said that tea was blended especially to suit the Manchester water.

The Pendleton Society was large enough to support its own bakery, dairy, slaughterhouse, and tailoring and dressmaking department. By 1910, within the Pendleton boundaries, it had 34 grocery shops, 25 butcher's shops, 6 draperies, 7 shops devoted exclusively to the sale of boots and shoes, 5 tailoring branches,

and 3 furnishing departments. It had established its 'Penny Bank' to encourage savings amongst young people, it supplied and delivered coal, and it made loans for the purchase of houses.

The Headquarters of the Pendleton Society were at Mill Street, Broughton Road. The advantage of becoming a member, was to share in the trading profits. To join the Society a prospective member had to visit the office and pay an entrance fee of

The Maypole Hotel and the buildings of the Pendleton Co-Operative Industrial Society, seen in this 1975 view, still survive on Broughton Road, though the latter is now occupied by Queens Park Motors.

one shilling (later reduced to sixpence), plus a further threepence for a copy of the rules. Each member of the Society was expected to hold at least three shares of £1 each, which could be paid in full on joining, or by instalments of three-shillings-and-fourpence per quarter. It was in a member's interests to shop only at the Co-Op, for purchases were recorded on a receipt, or 'check,' from which the 'divi' (dividend) could be collected once a quarter.

Those who went to work for the Co-Op usually started as 'Check Boys,' reckoning-up the check papers, and were later posted to the various branches. As the Society developed, it instituted its own education committee, established guilds for the ladies, convalescent homes, funeral department, travel agency and motor coach garage. When housewives talked of shopping at 'The Stores,' they meant the Co-Op.

But by the time of the centenary in 1960, trade had fallen away. Competition from supermarkets was blamed by some for the decline, as branches were closed as economy measures, and moves began for the eventual amalgamation with the Manchester & Salford Society.

_____ *Don Lingard*

The Pendleton Co-Operative Industrial Society was a local institution. In the 1930s and '40s it touched most of the families in Pendleton and Broughton. Other parts of the district were served by the Manchester & Salford Society, although many Salford families shopped 'over the border.'

Pendleton Co-Op could supply all needs. Its branches included grocery, footwear, outfitting (both ladies' and gents'), furniture, hardware, radio and electrical, butchery, and greengrocery. It provided coal and milk, delivered to your door. It had a laundry service, with collections and deliveries, a funeral service, and, during the war, it even ran a Youth Club.

You had to be a 'member' of the Society to benefit from the dividend, or 'divi' as it was known, and nearly every housewife was a member. On the purchase of any item from the Co-Op, on quoting the membership number, a customer received a 'check,' a little strip of gummed paper with the amount written on by the shop assistant. The 'check' was then stuck on a sheet, which, when full, could be taken to the nearest store, where it was totalled up and exchanged for a new, blank sheet. On Quarter Day, the 'divi' was paid out in the large hall at the Central Branch in Broughton Road. Hundreds of people would be there, queueing to receive their cash after first showing their pass-books. My mother's 'divi' always seemed to be used to pay the gas bill. Sometimes, the dividend would be as high as three shillings in the pound on all purchases, which was very good considering the bank interest rate was no more than 3%.

Pendleton Co-Op had large shops in prime positions on every main street of the area. Its buildings were amongst the smartest and best-kept, and most of them are standing today, some nearly 100 years old. The impressive hall above the Central store in Broughton Road could be hired for weddings, political meetings, exhibitions, amateur dramatics, or whatever, and at Christmas time there was always a Toy Fair. Just after the 1939-45 War, when the television service had been resumed in the London area only, Pendleton Co-Op arranged a demonstration of a broadcast from Crystal Palace. I, along with several hundred others in that hall, just managed to catch a glimpse of the tiny black-and-white screen. Another well-attended meeting in 1945 was to hear Charles Royle, one of the newly-elected Salford M.P.s, lecturing on the workings of Parliament.

If you worked for the Co-Op, it was considered that you were very lucky and were set-up with a job for life. My father was a milkman with the

Society. He worked seven days a week for 50 weeks in the year, including all Bank Holidays, and had only two weeks annual leave. In his time, milk was delivered by horse-drawn cart. At 6.00 a.m. he would collect his horse from the stables in Cheltenham Street, lead it to the dairy in Ford Lane, hitch it to the 'milk float' (cart), load the milk churns, together with supplies of cream and eggs, and then set off on his rounds. People were trusting in those days, and they would leave their jugs on the doorsteps, with little brass tokens underneath. Milk cost fourpence a pint, and the tokens could be purchased at the Co-Op shops. The milkman had to carry metal measures, with which to ladle out half-pints or pints, but later bottles with cardboard tops came into use. On finishing his round, my father would drive back to the dairy, unhitch and park the cart, and then take his horse to the stables, where it had to be groomed, fed, and watered. The stables were always very interesting for a small boy. There were two tiers of stalls, and the name of the horse was displayed above each stall. In the yard, there were forges, with farriers shoeing horses. In the early post-war years, electric battery-powered floats came into use, other delivery vehicles became motorised, and the horses disappeared forever.

The Co-Op sold nearly everything, and many of the goods were manufactured by the Co-Operative Wholesale Society (C.W.S.), noted for quality. The business of shopping was different – hours seemed to pass whilst waiting behind other customers, who would give their lists of groceries to the white-aproned assistants. The assistants would take down various items from the well-stocked shelves, weigh and put some products into paper bags, cut butter from great slabs and pat it into shape with wooden 'paddles,' slice the bacon, weigh and pack the 'King Edwards' ($1^1/_2$d per pound), and then reckon up the bill whilst packing the shopping basket. Not a calculator or shopping trolley in sight! The Pendleton Co-Op thrived and survived for over a hundred years, until competition forced amalgamation with the larger Manchester & Salford Society. Many of the buildings still exist, sometimes adapted for other uses, though their origin can often be detected from the Society's title incorporated into the stonework.

_____ *Mrs. H. Poynton*

When I was young, everything came from the Co-Op – bread, greengrocery, coal, even our first radio ! My sister and I sat for almost the whole of one Saturday, waiting for that radio to be delivered. What a thrilling day that was! As I grew older, and got married, I carried on the tradition of shopping with the Co-Op, saving the 'divi' sheets, and then going to draw the money on a certain date. This always came in handy for shoes for the children.

A Pianist for the Silent Films

Mrs. B. Rainger

When the 'talkies' came, pianists were no longer required in the cinemas.

Before the 1914-18 War, my mother was a Sunday School teacher at St.Peter's Church, Swinton. In addition to her regular job as a sales assistant in the Silversmiths' Department at Baxendale & Company, in Miller Street, Manchester, she also gave piano lessons. It was not long before she was asked to become the regular pianist for the Infants' Sunday School, which was housed in an old building in Brackley Street, Swinton. She enjoyed teaching the Sunday classes and playing the hymns, and I still have in my possession a rather tattered book containing 'Notes For Lessons,' which, to me, seemed rather complicated, but she used to assure me that once you were used to the system, understanding grew.

The Sunday School teachers also attended the main Church Services, and at this time, one of the church members, Mr. Belshaw, was the Manager of the Little Moss Empire Cinema, in Upper Sutherland Street, off Chorley Road, Swinton. To give it its proper title, the 'Moss Electric Empire' was the first 'picture palace' to have been built in Swinton, and had opened for the showing of silent films in September 1911. Mr. Belshaw asked my mother if she would play the piano to accompany the silent films then showing at the 'Little Moss.' The aim of the pianist was to match the music with the mood of the film at any given moment. For example, she would play 'Crescendo' at exciting parts of the story, or fast, slow, romantic, dreamy, etc., as required. I possess two much-used copies of 'Star Folios,' which contain music to meet all needs.

The titles of the various pieces are an indication of when or where they might be used - 'The Waves,' 'The Caliph Of Baghdad,' and so on.

When I was 10 years old, I attended Pendleton High School, and used to travel by tramcar from Swinton to the top of Langworthy Road. From that point, my friends and I were accustomed to taking a short cut across a croft to reach Eccles Old Road, but one morning we were surprised to find that our usual route had been blocked. We discovered that a cinema was to be built there, and we were intrigued to watch the daily progress as the 'Ambassador' reached completion in 1928. One of the first films to be shown was called 'Blossom Time.' My father took me to see this film, and I was amazed to find that the whole of the cinema foyer had been decorated with branches of pink and white blossom - a memorable occasion. Violet Carson, who later became famous as a television actress, made her debut playing the piano in this cinema, and I remember the thrill of seeing the cinema organ appearing, as if by magic, from beneath the floor when Reginald Liversedge played.

Years later, I had the pleasure of acting as bridesmaid at my best friend's wedding. The reception was held in the restaurant of the Ambassador Cinema.

*The 'Ambassador'
Cinema in Langworthy
Road, now a bingo
hall, opened in 1928.*

The "Ragged School"

George Harrison

On a recent visit to the Local History Library, a box marked "Windsor Institute" opened up the floodgates of memory. Although the "Windsor Institute and Pendleton Ragged School" (to give it its full title) opened in West George Street in 1858, my acquaintance with it dated only from 1924, at which time it was probably at the height of its influence.

Sunday evenings saw hundreds of children attending the services. Girls entered by the right-hand door, boys by the left – complete segregation! We faced the platform, on which were the Superintendent, with the members of the choir ranged behind him, and, higher up, Alfred Williams at the organ. And what rousing 'Sankey & Moody' hymns we sang, and with what gusto! ('Dare, dare, dare to do right; Dare, dare, dare to be true!') All without hymn books, of course. Instead, the Superintendent operated a metal-framed contraption, which contained a series of roller-blinds on which were printed in large letters the words of the hymn to be sung.

And what trouble this device gave at times! The rolls sometimes refused to be unrolled, and at other times sprang back up in mid-sentence. The Superintendent I remember best was John Paul McDougall, former Mayor of Salford, and a member, I believe, of the flour-milling family.

But Tuesday nights were the nights! Tuesday was when we had the 'penny pictures,' two hours of sheer delight in the company of Hoot Gibson, Tom Mix, Charlie Chase, and so many other old favourites of the silent film days. All in black-and-white, of course, and no sound, but how we wished the week away until Tuesday came round again! It was Laurie Gannon, I think, who ran the cinema shows. They were attended by hundreds of children from far and wide. Projector breakdowns were frequent, and were always accompanied by the stamping of feet and whistling when the lights came on.

Christmas was always special at the 'Ragged.' All those who earned a ticket by regular attendance (an 'S' card was duly stamped as we entered on Sunday evenings) were invited to turn up at 9.00am on Christmas morning for the Christmas Breakfast. We each had to bring a cup. On entry, everyone was presented with a bag containing assorted things to eat. Included, if I remember correctly, were a meat pie, a sandwich, and a cake. I cannot recall whether we had our eats before or after the singing of carols, but, whenever it was, it was certainly enjoyed, and probably represented the only decent breakfast that some of those children had during the whole year. Later in the proceedings, we were usually visited by the Mayor, wearing his chain of office. He always said a few words to us, wished everyone a Merry Christmas, and then disappeared, no doubt to grace other similar functions around the city. At the end of the breakfast, we each received a toy, together with a bag containing an apple and an orange. Truly, it was a memorable day in our calendar.

Another great event was the annual day's outing to Heaton Park. This, again, was by ticket awarded for regular attendance. What a sight it must have been to see hundreds of children marching up West George Street to board a fleet of special trams waiting on Windsor Bridge. When all were safely on board, we clanged away down Broad Street, Frederick Road, Great Clowes Street, Great Cheetham Street, Leicester Road, Middleton Road, right into the Park itself. The journey seemed to take hours, but in reality must only have been about 30 minutes, but then the joy of being free to roam the enchanted acres of Heaton Park, with a trip in the motor boat round the lake being thrown in for good measure. This was followed by a sandwich tea, and then, after more fun and games, bedraggled and weary, but blissfully happy youngsters climbed aboard the waiting trams (with a box of sweets courtesy of the Tramways Department) for the homeward ride back to the 'Ragged.'

Many other things about the 'Ragged' come to mind, but what I liked least was the annual 'Procession Of Witness' around the neighbourhood. No doubt the little girls in their white dresses thoroughly enjoyed hanging on to a banner string, but to me, and many other boys, there was a sense of embarrassment as we trailed along in our Sunday-best at the end of a procession. We always seemed to be miles away from the Windsor Prize Band, blowing away with gusto at the head of the column. The cul-mination of the 'Walk' was a gathering in Unwin Square, where a service, attended by hundreds, was held in the open air. Afterwards, we walked back to the 'Ragged' and welcome relief! During my time, a new banner was obtained, a marvellous colourful affair, which bore a picture of the Windsor Institute. We were told that the banner had been specially embroidered in France.

I have already mentioned the 'S' cards used for recording Sunday attendances. They were very important documents if you wanted a ticket for a treat. The attendance records were kept in an office on the right-hand side of the platform, and were scrutinised weekly to detect any back-sliders. If anyone dared to miss a couple of Sundays, mother would have a visit from a tubby old gentleman called Mr.Crosby. He was the 'Sick Visitor,' a wonderful old character, who did his rounds faith-fully for many years.

Much more could be said about an organisation which continued its good work until 1966, when a compulsory purchase order was served because of impending redevelopment of the area. This order forced the doors to close for the last time. Better pens than mine could doubtless tell more interesting stories. My association with the 'Ragged' was severed as long ago as 1932, but I recall with great pleasure the many happy hours spent there as a child.

The Windsor Institute, or 'Ragged School,' was situated at the end of a gloomy street, but was a centre of social and religious life in

Recollections of a Home Guard, 1942-44

James A. Grimshaw

Today's image of Britain's Home Guard in the 1939-45 War is largely the one created by the television series "Dad's Army," that of a small group of ill-equipped ancient warriors preparing to resist the might of the invading Wermacht. Whatever the truth of this in the early days, and there was undoubtedly a great deal of chaos in 1940, little has been written of the later years when the Allies were preparing to take the offensive, and the role of the Home Guard was considerably expanded. This is not the place to tell that story, nor am I the one to attempt to do so. A few personal memories may, however, shed a little light on the subject in so far as it affected Salfordians.

In the spring of 1942 the Home Guard launched a recruiting drive, with 'press gangs' roaming the streets in an effort to persuade any non-uniformed male to join their ranks. There was no apparent reason for this upsurge in activity, and it seemed rather irrelevant to the prevailing situation, for the German armies had more than enough problems in Russia and were most unlikely to try to invade Britain at that time. In such circumstances, I was content to continue my fire-picket duties in Trafford Park, so I declined all invitations to join the Home Guard. Others must have been of like mind, and the recruiting campaign presumably failed to attract sufficient volunteers, because shortly afterwards I was 'directed' into the Home Guard. Thus it was that at the age of 19, I found myself on parade (along with some 1500 others, one evening per week and every Sunday morning) in a field at the rear of houses in Lancaster Road and Oxford Road. It soon became clear that our allotted task was to take overmanning of the adjoining anti-aircraft battery from the regular army. The battery occupied the area which is now the Duncan Mathieson playing fields, just off Lancaster Road.

Sunday mornings were mostly spent 'square bashing,' with the occasional route march or church parade to add a touch of variety. More specific training was carried out in the evenings. I can remember a former cinema in Liverpool Road, Eccles, having a rocket projector installed for instruction purposes, although I cannot name the cinema. We were also instructed in the use of the rifle (necessary for guard duties) and in the use of the STEN gun, which was rather pointless as we were unlikely to be involved in street fighting. Other useless lectures included those on aircraft recognition, for we would be manning the battery only at night.

Came the great day when we were to collect our uniforms. Everything was available in the right sizes except boots, when, instead of my small 9s, I was offered the choice of a pair of small 8s or large 12s. The joys of 'square bashing' on long grass in army boots three sizes too big are beyond description, and can only be experienced !

All projector drill was carried out using dummy ammunition, practice firing with live rounds taking place on the coastal range at Freshfields, the range being sited, with typical military disregard for other services, on the direct landing approach to the nearby Woodvale airfield.

Before many weeks had passed, most of the army personnel had moved out, leaving behind only a command-post team, together with some armourers and a sufficient number of troops to provide daytime security. The Home Guard took over the night-time manning of the battery, which comprised 64 rocket projectors, each capable of firing a salvo of two rockets to a height of 20,000 feet. The rockets were about four feet long, weighed 60 pounds each, and had a warhead containing $4\frac{1}{2}$ pounds of high explosive. About 200 officers and men per night were required to man the site, with two men to each projector, a non-commissioned officer for every four projectors, and an officer to every sixteen, plus guards and, later, command-post staff. With a one-night-in-eight rota, and some six batteries operational in the Manchester gun-defended area, it can be seen that the operation was anything but small, with some 10,000 men involved. There was no friction between the Home Guard and the Royal Artillery gunners who remained on site, although some of the regular army officers were less than enthusiastic about the take-over.

Taking over an established site had the advantages of proper sleeping accommodation in Nissen huts, together with excellent messing arrangements. The ATS cooks remained in charge of catering, and eating like soldiers once a week proved a welcome bonus at a time of strict food rationing.

When the Home Guard eventually took on the Command Post duties, I was recruited on to the 'plotting team.' Initially, targets were plotted on a vertical screen, with co-ordinates received by telephone from the Manchester Gun Operations Room, which was situated in the basement of a large house in Park Lane, Broughton. Soon, however, we were provided with a plotting room and a semi-automatic plotter at the anti-aircraft gun site located behind Peel Green cemetery. This site had its own radar equipment, and duties there entailed reporting first at Lancaster Road, then being taken by army transport to Peel Green, from where we were returned to Lancaster Road the following morning. This would have been fine, except that one of our number had to be at work in Horwich by 7.00am, so we all had to be up at 5.00am. This did nothing to enhance our popularity with the cooks, who had to rise even earlier in order to prepare our breakfasts. Consequently, no one was sorry when our colleague found some other way of spending his nights. At that period, the Peel Green battery of 3.7 inch guns was manned by men of the Royal Artillery, though I believe that later this site was also taken over by the Home Guard.

Trips to Peel Green ended when our own site near Lancaster Road was also equipped with radar. The new equipment was located in the area bounded by Hereford and Winchester Roads, and was operated by soldiers from REME. Older residents of the district may remember the barbed wire fences and the uncompromising 'Trespassers Will Be Shot' notices.

Being in the Command Post, where I was eventually promoted to sergeant in charge of the plotting team, was regarded as a 'cushy job' when compared with manning a projector, or being out on guard in winter weather. On the debit side, however, telephones had to be manned all night, the Command Post team had to 'stand to' whenever enemy aircraft were active, even if this activity was over distant parts of the country, and on several occasions long night exercises were conducted tracking and 'engaging' friendly aircraft.

In Salford, our weapons were never fired in anger, although on one or two occasions the prospect came very close. Nevertheless, it would be an understatement to say that everyone was surprised when the order came for the Home Guard to 'stand down' on the 3rd December 1944. The war was still far from won, and the Luftwaffe was still capable of springing a few surprises, including the V-1 rocket attack aimed at Manchester on the 24th December 1944.

Fifty years on, no trace remains of the battery, but if, round about 10.00 am, the Sunday-morning footballers on the Duncan Mathieson field were to listen to the shouts coming from the touch-line, maybe they would hear an echo of the voice of the sergeant-major bringing the 1500 men of Z 101 battery to attention.

Salford

Ted O'Brien

They say
There is no beauty
Anywhere
In Salford.

They say,
That grass and trees
Are never seen
In such a mean
And dirty place
As Salford.

They say
That all the streets
Are dark
And narrow;
That the Classic Slum
Is to be seen
In every part
Of Salford.

I know
Where there are roads
To travel,
Tree-lined,
And blossom-scented
In the Spring
In Salford.

I know
Where there are parks
To be
At ease,
Where bands once played
For Lowry's entertainment,
In Salford.

I know
Where there are woods
To roam,
To hear sweet singing birds,
Day long
In Salford.

They say,
But
I know

St James' Church Bells and Sandy Lane

Lily Hodson

One of my earliest memories as a child was of hearing the bell for the Angelus at St.James' Church, Pendleton. I lived with my family close by in Binns Street. The bell rang at 6.00am, 12.00 noon, and 6.00pm every day. Life seemed to be ruled by the bell – lunch time out of school; tea time, Dad coming home from work, and the instruction, "Go and watch for him."

The bells, and references to them, stayed with me for a long time. When I started work in 1934 at Metropolitan Vickers in Trafford Park, to get me up Mam would shout, "The bells have gone, and the man with the clogs has passed." The man with the clogs would be going to work at Pendleton Pit.

It was the same even on a Sunday. I can hear Mam saying at dinner time, "There's the bell, and I haven't got the potatoes on !" Mam even told me that the St. James's bell was ringing when I was born on the 1st May 1920. It was a wonder I wasn't named 'Angela,' but I am told that the midwife said I was "fair as a lily," so that name was chosen.

When I was at school, I was friendly with a girl named Mary, who lived at the Eccles Old Road end of Sandy Lane. There were two big houses and a Lodge near white gates, masses of mature trees, and birds singing, which made me feel as if I was in the country. My friend lived in the first house, which was let off into rooms for families, although I never saw other people there. It was always very quiet, and very clean, as a lady was employed to clean and polish floors in the hall. On the ground floor, there were large rooms, with big Adam-style fireplaces and shuttered windows, which must have been the sitting and dining rooms when the original owners lived there. There were also French windows which led on to a flight of steps and the garden. The hall, staircase, bathroom and toilets, all with mahogany panels, seemed wonderful to me. At the bottom of a small flight of stairs lay the kitchen, and once Mary took me in and I was impressed by the row of bells on the wall.

Another flight of steps led to another door on the Old Road. I think this second door had been the tradesmen's entrance. The big garden was full of rhododendron bushes. Nowadays, when I hear the blackbirds singing, I think about that garden in Sandy Lane and Mary. I didn't know they were blackbirds then – only birds!

The Salford Fire Brigade

Bill Woods

The Salford Fire Brigade was responsible for a revolution in fire-fighting, features of which remain today. For centuries, the 'Porte Mote Court' governed the administration of Salford, and in the sixteenth century the records of that court stated, "A provision of Watch and Fire Protection should be provided. Later, on the 11th November 1615, it was decided "to purchase 12 buckets of lether, 2 hookes, 2 longe ladders, to be kept in a convenient and suitable place, as suitable fittings for preventing of fire." The convenient and suitable place proved to be the tower of Trinity Chapel, later to become Sacred Trinity Church. Thus, for many years Sacred Trinity tower became Salford's fire-fighting headquarters.

Sacred Trinity Church bell was used as the town's fire alarm, but with the vast growth and extension of the built-up area in the period of the Industrial Revolution, the two small, manually-operated fire 'engines' housed there, proved insufficient. They would have had no chance of containing fires in the four or five-storey mills being built along the banks of the Irwell. The ineptitude of the part-time firemen, together with the difficulties posed by their antiquated equipment, meant that fire protection was inadequate and inefficient. Yet the powers of the Police Commissioners (under the Police Act of 1792) made little impact. Perhaps the war with Revolutionary France, subsequent food riots, and industrial distress, may be offered as excuses for the laxity of the Commissioners. Whatever the reason, the records show that the Fire Brigade consisted only of 12 firemen, a 'conductor,' and two fire engines.

By 1800, the Fire Station had moved to Fire Engine House, Police Yard, Harding's Buildings, Chapel Street. The firemen were paid for attendance, and were equipped with "coats, japanned hats, and staff or javelins." In 1825 reference is made to William Rose, Horse Dealer, of Chapel Street, being promoted to the post of Superintendent. In 1830 the Salford Improvement Act gave the local authority powers to provide and maintain a suitable fire brigade and equipment, and on the 24th June of that year John Thompson was appointed 'Conductor' of the Brigade. Thompson was followed in quick succession by Joseph Jeffries, Joshua Holt, and a Mr. Darling.

In 1834 the Fire Station moved again, this time to premises on Chapel Street, "next door to the Lamb Inn and opposite the Albert Vaults." By this date, the Brigade had a strength of 15 firemen. Their uniforms consisted of "trousers and coat of Russia duck, with embossed button bearing the town's coat-of-arms, star of office on their coats, and a belt of leather, staff and torch, and leather hat - varnished." As late as 1835, even though the station had moved twice, the Sacred Trinity bell was still used as the alrm signal.

By 1847 the Fire Station was located on West Market Street, which is now enclosed between the Bexley Square Town Hall and Annexe. At this date, there were 34 firemen and the Conductor. By 1860, Broughton and Pendleton had merged with

90

Salford, but Broughton still maintained its own highly-efficient volunteer fire brigade, and Pendleton also had an independent brigade housed in Police Street, immediately behind the old Pendleton Town Hall on Broughton Road.

In 1874 the Ford Street headquarters of the Salford Fire Brigade was erected, and two horse-drawn 'steamers' (water pumps powered by steam boiler) were purchased in 1875 and 1878. Then Salford made a most unwise decision to merge the Fire Brigade with the Police Force, the fire-fighters thus becoming the Police Fire Brigade. Recognising the increasing danger from fire, and the great area to be covered, it was agreed to provide hose-carts and scaling ladders at the Police Stations at Silk Street, Great Cheetham Street, Moor Lane, Irlams O' Th' Height, Trafford Road, and Regent Road. The Salford Fire Chief was a Mr. Willis, but in 1891 he applied for, and was duly appointed to the position of Chief Fire Officer for the City of Liverpool.

A postcard issued in commemoration of the Chief Officer of the Salford Fire Brigade, Albert Bentley, who died in 1905. The Fire Station opened in 1903 was equipped to his specifications. It is now the 'Viewpoint Gallery.'

So it was that in 1891 perhaps the wisest and most far-sighted decision was made to appoint Albert Bentley, then aged 31, to be the 'Superintendent' (i.e. Chief Officer) of the Salford Fire Brigade. Bentley had been a professional fireman since his 18th birthday, and before coming to Salford was Deputy Chief of the Bradford Fire Brigade. Almost overnight, the Salford Fire Brigade became celebrated throughout Britain. Albert Bentley proved to be a brilliant man, a born leader, and a man of vision. He converted the fly-ladder into a telescopic fire-escape. Until this time, volunteers had to run the fly-ladders along the streets on six-feet-diameter wheels, but Bentley altered the horse-drawn fire-engines in such a way that they could carry the wheeled telescopic escape.

Being dissatisfied with the speed of turn-out, Bentley invented and patented an electrically-operated harnessing device, and was able to reduce the time taken to have the fire-appliances on the road to a mere 50 seconds. He argued for an increase in man-power, and had the strength increased to 28 firemen. By 1900, he had obtained permission to build one of the finest fire-stations in the country, together with the firemen's houses immediately behind in Albion Square. Originally designed for horse-drawn fire appliances (open harnesses hung from the ceiling, arranged for rapid turn-out), the new 'Central Fire Station' opened in September 1903, and was later easily adapted for motor fire engines. Fortunately, these buildings, together with the additional engine-houses on the flanks, survive today, though converted for other uses.

When Bentley came to Salford, the water pressure in the mains was most unsatisfactory for his purposes. Therefore, he gave orders for the construction of eleven underground tanks, connected to the mains, but each holding a reserve of 500 gallons. They were positioned at strategic points: New Bridge Street; Irwell Street; Flat Iron Market Place; Brown Street ; Adelphi Street ; Regent Road ; Ordsall

Lane; Cross Lane; Greengate; Dickenson Street; and Cobden Street. Bentley also gained authority to appoint to his staff wheelwrights, blacksmiths, carpenters, coach builders, painters, and electricians, all with the aim of keeping equipment in the best possible working order. Fire officers, members of Watch Committees, and councillors came to Salford from all parts of the country to inspect and gain ideas from Bentley's organisation.

Albert Bentley died at his post in 1905, aged 45, having devoted his career to the improvement of fire-fighting services. Perhaps it would be a fitting honour if Albion Square was to be re-named Albert Bentley Square.

Salford was also fortunate in having located within its boundaries several famous fire engineering companies. One of these was John Morris and Sons, whose founder had invented the male/female connecting joint for hose-pipes, used throughout the world. Another company was Reddaway & Sons, inventors of a method of weaving canvas hose which eliminated the possibility of leakage. The firm of Thomas Hollins, of Oldfield Road, had been manufacturers of fire-fighting appliances since 1816.

The greatest testing time for the Salford Brigade and its partners, the A.F.S. (Auxiliary Fire Service), was during the Second World War. Between the wars, the Salford Brigade had grown to cover not only Salford, but also Swinton, Pendlebury, and Prestwich. Its telephone number, BLA 2222, was well-known throughout the area. In the blitz of the 22nd/23rd December 1940, resources were stretched to their limit. One great conflagration had 100 pumps in attendance, and there were 36 other very serious fires (each demanding 50 pumps), as well as hundreds of smaller outbreaks, for which the assistance of volunteer fire-fighters was required. Totally overwhelmed by the fierce attack, most of the eight fire-engines then stationed at Albion Square had been sent to fires which were raging betwen Chapel Street and the River Irwell, and which spread later to the coal storage yards by Salford Railway Station. Within ten minutes, the Brigade had lost its Morris Magirus turntable machine, its crew members either killed or badly injured. The water mains were broken by high-explosive bombs, but Albert Bentley's inventive genious saved the day, as two 'Big Reds' (1000 gallon per minute pumps) were able to tap the underground tanks and mains on Albert Bridge corner and at Flat Iron Market.

A convoy of no fewer than 42 fire-engines from the West and East Ridings of Yorkshire struggled over the Pennines to assist. They reached the Central Fire Station in Albion Square via Agecroft Bridge and Bolton Road, the only passable route, arriving at 1.00 a.m. on the 23rd December 1940. Never in his wildest dreams could Albert Bentley have envisaged such a scene in the Fire Station he built.

In 1923 the Salford Fire Brigade invested in a fire engine which had the latest motorised turntable with an extending ladder. It is seen here in the fire station forecourt, in front of the side garages which housed the auxiliary vehicles.

Salford's 'Merry Widow'

Robert Bracken

Miss Lily Elsie, Salford's own 'Merry Widow.'

She was the idol of the theatre world. Women wanted to be like her, and wore the 'Merry Widow' hat, which became the fashion of the day. Her photograph appeared on picture postcards, chocolate boxes, and advertisements. The young Winston Churchill was once heard to say, "It is unthinkable to see 'The Merry Widow' without Lily Elsie.

'Lily Elsie' was actually Elsie Cotton, born 8th April 1886 in the Ordsall area of Salford. She was brought up by her grandparents, Mr. & Mrs. Hodder, at 16 Trafford Road. Her show-business career began as a child entertainer in local concert parties. When only nine years of age, she was in demand for concerts at the London & North Western Hotel on Cross Lane, which was situated close to Cross Lane Station (on the London & North Western Railway) opposite the military barracks. The hotel was managed at that time by Mrs. Sarah Higham, whose son, Sam, was an organiser of popular concerts. Young Elsie was then billed as 'Little Elsie,' and as part of her act would give impersonations of favourite music hall artists, such as Vesta Tilley and Harry Lauder.

Sam Higham wrote a sketch entitled "There'll Come A Time One Day," in which he and Elsie acted. This became very popular, and the pair performed it across the road at the then new Regent Theatre (later the 'Palace') in a charity benefit for the manager. The sketch was repeated at the 'Prince Of Wales' theatre in Liverpool Street, and Elsie came to the attention of Richard Flanagan, manager of the old Queen's Theatre in Bridge Street,

Manchester. In 1897 Flanagan engaged her to play the part of Princess Mirza in 'The Arabian Nights.' It was said that 'Little Elsie' made an ideal princess. Her acting and 'perfect pose' were much admired. At this theatre, she took over the title role in the pantomime 'Little Red Riding Hood.'

Theatre managers competed for her services. Mr. Pitt Hardacre was successful in booking her to appear over at the Gaiety Theatre, and afterwards she went on tour. But Elsie was afraid of London, and would travel only in company with her grandmother, Mrs. Hodder. Her first musical was at the Strand Theatre in 'The Chinese Honeymoon.' Back in Manchester, at the Queen's Theatre she acted in 'See, See,' before receiving an invitation from George Edwards to accompany him to Vienna to see the musical by Franz Lehar, 'The Merry Widow.'

Edwards wanted Elsie to take the leading part in his London production. At first she declined the offer, as she felt unable to cope with the dancing, but eventually, and reluctantly, consented to appear. So, in 1907 'The Merry Widow' came to London's Leicester Square. Theatre-lovers queued for the first night, hoping to gain a seat, and there was much excitement in the theatre as the audience waited for the curtain to rise. When 'Lily Elsie' appeared, there was a murmur of admiration, and her dazzling beauty seemed to capture hearts at once. When she sang and danced, the whole house was enchanted. The famous waltz was repeated over and over again, and still the audience cried for more encores.

Enjoying tremendous success, Elsie remained unspoilt. She was 26 years of age when she married a millionaire's son, Ian Bullough, of Accrington. The wedding took place at All Saints Church, Ennismore Gardens, London, in November 1911. Elsie was given away by the Hon. Charles Russell, who had been the unsuccessful Liberal candidate for South Salford in the 1910 election, after Hilaire Belloc had resigned. On the marriage certificate,

Elsie's mother, Elsie Cotton, was recorded as Elsie Barrett, a lodging-house keeper in Salford, and her father, the late William Thomas Cotton, as being a former theatrical manager from Wortley, near Leeds.

Elsie retired from the stage and enjoyed married life for many years. Unhappily, her husband became a serious alcoholic, and went through a number of bad patches before he and Elsie finally separated. The strain had affected Elsie, too, and she retired into a nursing home. She died on the 16th December 1962, aged 76.

The Sunday School girls make a splendid sight in their new dresses. From the other side of the street, the three banners read correctly, left to right, 'God Is Love.'

Salford's Special Constabulary

W.C. Turner

Assistant Chief Commandant, Greater Manchester Police Special Constabulary

The Special Constabulary is a volunteer, part-time, unpaid, uniformed reserve to the regular police force. Its origins are thought to stem from Saxon times, when one man in ten, the 'Tything Man,' was appointed to see that peace was kept amongst his neighbours and, when necessary, to pursue offenders and deliver them into the King's Justice. This developed into the 'Watch and Ward' system, and later, during the reign of Charles II, it became usual to 'swear in' Special Constables who were required to serve for one year to assist Constables when required.

The modern Special Constabulary springs from an Act of 1831, which enabled Magistrates to appoint officers if disorder was anticipated, and if the number of regular constables was thought insufficient to preserve the peace. The Special Constables were to have all the powers of the regular officers, and were to be armed with staves and other necessary equipment.

The first recorded instance of Special Constables being appointed in the Salford area was in 1834, when Abraham Driver, Deputy Constable of Broughton (then a separate township) accompanied 23 men to be sworn in at New Bailey Prison. In his diary, Driver recorded that each man was issued with a numbered staff. In the following year, 22 special officers, most of them the same men as in 1834, were sworn in, suggesting that they were being appointed on an annual basis, and not because of any temporary emergency.

Salford must also have made similar appointments in the same period, for in 1836, in reports of presentations to John Diggles, Deputy Constable of Salford, it is recorded that there were five 'divisions' of Special Constables. In 1844, when Salford attained the status of a Borough, with a Watch Committee, the Salford Borough Police was formed, with Diggles as the first Chief Constable. Unhappily, his period in office proved to be short, for both he and his deputy, Superintendent John Ward, were dismissed in the following year because of irregularities in payments to constables for court appearances.

The Special Constables were frequently called into action to protect life and property during periods of industrial and social unrest in Queen Victoria's time. During the 1860s, the Fenian Society and the Irish Republican Brotherhood instigated a campaign of violence, ostensibly in favour of Irish independence, and in 1867 two 'Fenians' were arrested in Manchester. Whilst being conveyed in a prison van in charge of Sergeant Brett, they were released by sympathisers, and the Sergeant was shot dead. Those responsible for the murder were later executed at the New Bailey Prison, and a commemorative staff, presented to Ged Shaw, who was on duty as a Salford Special at the New Bailey, is still in existence.

In 1911 the area saw several fierce industrial disputes, principally the Salford Dock Strike, when officers were called in from other forces to help keep control of the situation. A national railway strike followed, and as it was not then possible to obtain outside assistance, the Chief Constable resorted to calling out the Special Constables. A total of 52 'Specials' were enrolled and deployed to guard railway lines and signal boxes, whilst the regular officers thus released were able to act as escorts to convoys of coal carts supplying the gas works and factories. When this particular dispute was resolved, it was revealed that the cost to the Borough of using the Special Constables amounted to only £53.

The outbreak of war in 1914 brought manpower problems for the regular police, many of whose officers were ex-servicemen who were recalled to the forces. The 'spy mania' which swept the country added to the difficulties, and Salford enlisted 227 Special Constables in 1914 to guard possible sabotage targets. The writer recalls being told (in 1950) by one of the 1914 'Specials' that he had been equipped with a 303 service rifle and a bandolier of ammunition for his first duty, which was to guard Trafford Bridge. A further Special Constabulary Act extended service for an indefinite period.

Major C. V. Godfrey, Chief Constable, inspecting the Salford Special Constabulary during the Second World War.

By 1915, Salford had a total of 610 'Specials,' 415 of whom were guarding factories engaged in war work, and 191 were carrying out police patrols in the city. The torpedoing of the Cunard liner 'Lusitania' in May 1915 sent a wave of anger throughout the country, which found expression in violence and attacks on the property of persons of German descent, or even those with German-sounding names. Salford was not immune, and the 'Specials' were deployed to protect property against mob attacks. In 1917, when King George V and Queen Mary visited the city, 300 'Specials' were on duty.

The period of indefinite service ended in 1919, when the Special Constabulary was stood down. Special Superintendent J.W. Willoughby, who commanded the Salford Special Constabulary throughout the war, was awarded an O.B.E. for his services. Those who had served prior to 1916 were presented with an emblazoned staff and an illuminated certificate, whilst those who had enrolled between 1916 and 1918 received the certificate only. King George V instituted the Special Constabulary Long Service Medal in 1919, to reward 3 years wartime service, or 9 years in peacetime. A bar is awarded for each additional 10 years service. Recipients have also to satisfy the Chief Constable as to their competence and training, as well as regularly and faithfully performing duty. After the 1914-18 war, some Police Authorities decided to maintain their Special Constabularies on a permanent basis, whilst others felt they lacked the necessary legal powers to do so, but the situation was regularised by an Act of 1923, which allowed the 'Specials' to remain as a permanent reserve force.

The Irish 'troubles' of the early 1920s saw 120 Special Constables on duty to deal with rioters. The next major problem was the General Strike of 1926, when there was great anxiety about the transport and distribution of food. To this end, no fewer than 226,000 Special Constables were appointed throughout the United Kingdon, Salford's share being 461. Their duties were to carry out day-to-day policing, whilst the regular force ensured that vital supplies of food, fuel and other services were maintained. Afterwards, in recognition of their valued contribution, the Chief Constable entertained the Salford 'Specials' to a Hot Pot Supper.

Prior to the Second World War, the municipal elections were held in November. In 1930, the date of polling day clashed with the Manchester November Handicap, the principal race of the Castle Irwell calendar. The demand placed upon resources could not be met by the regular force, and the Chief Constable decided that the policing of polling stations should be undertaken by the Special Constabulary. The experiment was a success, and from that date 'Specials' have assisted the regular force at both local and general elections.

Sadly, in 1934, as a result of financial constraints during the trade depression, the Salford Council decided to save money by disbanding the Special Constabulary. But by 1938 it was feared that Hitler's aggressive policies would lead to war, and that in any future conflict, Britain would suffer heavy air attack. Parliament required local authorities to create an Air Raid Precautions organisation, and in Salford the chosen executive officer was the Chief Constable, Major C.V. Godfrey. Amongst other suggested measures, he called for the re-activation of the Special Constabulary, with a strength of 200 volunteers - men between 30 and 60 years of age. The volunteers were trained in law and police duties, anti-gas precautions, first aid, and foot drill, and by January 1939 the first batch had been 'sworn in' under the command of Captain R.L. Busby, who in civilian life was Company Secretary of the Manchester Racecourse Company.

On the outbreak of war, Captain Busby was given the title of Commandant, with the rank of Special Superintendent, Walter Stonex was appointed Deputy Commandant, and the strength increased to 300 men. The 'Specials' were divided into three divisions, 'A', 'B' and 'C', to co-incide with the regular force based on the Divisional Headquarters at Regent Road, Langworthy Road, and Park Lane, Broughton. Each section had a Divisional Commandant, with the rank of Special Inspector, and each had a complement of 7 Special Sergeants. During the 'Christmas Blitz' of 1940, the 'Specials,' along with the other A.R.P. services, performed their duties superbly. Four men were injured, and two, Special Sergeant Edward Ross (British Empire Medal) and Special Constable William Beckett (King's Commendation), received awards for gallantry.

Captain Busby died in 1941 and was succeeded by his Deputy, Walter Stonex. George James May, the 'C' Divisional Commandant, became the new Deputy Commandant. In 1942 and again in 1944 the Special Constabulary took over the policing of the city for 24 hours to enable the officers of the regular force to have a rest day. This was an expression of the confidence felt by the Chief Constable in the 'Specials,' and one which illustrated the high standard of efficiency they had reached. At least nine officers received the Chief Constable's commendation for their work during the war.

From September 1941 registration for some form of service in the Civil Defence organisations had been compulsory. Prior to that date, service as a Special Constable had been entirely voluntary, and on the 1st July 1945 the Corps was returned to voluntary status, and its numbers considerably reduced. In 1949 it was reorganised into two divisions, 'North' and 'South,' in line with the regular force. Its duties continued to be normal street patrols, race meetings at Castle Irwell, processions, elections, and any other events which called for increased police manpower. Walter Stonex died in 1958, and was succeeded by G.J. May, who was to command the Salford City Special Constabulary for the remainder of its existence.

In 1960 the Special Constabulary received a new uniform, changing its traditional 'choker' tunics for the modern style. George May received an M.B.E. in the 1964 Honours List for his services to the Special Constabulary.

In 1968, as a result of recommendations made by a Royal Commission, Salford City Poilce was amalgamated with the Manchester City Police to become the Manchester and Salford Police. The final act of the old force took place on the Castle Irwell Racecourse on Sunday, the 31st March 1968, when the regular force and the Special Constabulary paraded for the last time, and were inspected by Her Majesty's Inspector of Constabulary, Sidney Lawrence, himself a former Salford police constable, and Superintendent of the 'A' Division during the blitz. The salute was taken by Alderman A.E. Clark, Mayor of Salford, and Mr. Lawrence. At the end of the ceremony, the Salford City Police marched off the parade ground and into history.

However, it was not the end of the Special Constabulary in the city. 'Specials' still support their regular colleagues as the 'F' Division of the Greater Manchester Police Special Constabulary, and still maintain the long tradition of service to the community in peace and war, good times and bad, fair weather and foul.

Commandants of the Special Constabulary in Salford since its reactivation in 1938

Salford City Police
R. L. Busby, M.C., O.B.E., J.P.	1938–1941
W. Stonex, M.B.E., J.P.	1941–1958
G. J. May, M.B.E.	1958–1968

Manchester and Salford Police
G. J. May, M.B.E.	April–August, 1968
W. C. Turner	1968–1974

Greater Manchester Police
W. C. Turner	1974–1988
G. Caulfield	1988–1989
W. Bebbington	1989–

The final parade of the Salford 'Specials' took place at Castle Irwell Racecourse on the 31st March 1968, when the Mayor of Salford and H.M. Inspector of Constabulary took the salute.

Salford Triplets of 1929

_____ *Jean Gilliland*

In 1929 Margaret Jones, wife of Reuben Jones, crane driver on Salford Docks, gave birth to triplets at their home in Lord Duncan Street, off Cross Lane, Salford. The babies, two girls and a boy, were named Edna (3½ lbs), Iris (2½ lbs) and Neville (4½ lbs). Iris was so small she was not expected to live - she was wrapped in cotton wool and fed with brandy and water. Mrs.Jones received a matinee coat for each child from the Mayor of Salford, and ten shillings for each triplet from the King's bounty. Were these three children Salford's first triplets ?

All three thrived. They attended West Liverpool Street Infants' School, St.Luke's Church on Liverpool Street, and Hodge Lane Mission. In 1933, Iris, Edna and Neville, together with their older sister Margaret, took part in the Mission's annual Whit Walk. Iris and Edna were dressed as twins, and all three girls carried bouquets provided by their mother's cousin, who had a florist's shop.

At the outbreak of war in 1939 the triplets were evacuated to Lancaster, where, for the first time, Neville was separated from the girls, when he was allocated to a different foster mother. His new

The Jones triplets, Iris, Edna, and Neville, with elder sister Margaret, dressed for Hodge Lane Mission Whit Walks in 1933.

family liked him so much that they wanted to adopt him, so Mrs. Jones went to Lancaster and brought all three back to Salford, where they remained.

Neville attended Tootal Road School, but Iris and Edna remained at West Liverpool Street Girls' School. The girls were identical, and people assumed they were twins. Only when they were leaving, did the Senior School teachers discover the existence of a brother.

The passing years have not diminished the strong family ties between the triplets. Although they now live in different parts of the country, they maintain regular links with each other by telephone and letter. Neville and his wife are now retired and live in Portesham, near Weymouth, Edna and her husband, who are also retired, live in Denton, Manchester. Iris, a widow for seventeen years, lives in Cleveleys, near Blackpool. Recently, the triplets were re-united in Cleveleys for the wedding of Iris's younger son. Margaret, the elder sister, married an American, and lives in Michigan, U.S.A., but she, too, keeps in touch with the triplets at regular intervals.

The Jones triplets in the playground of West Liverpool Street Infants' School about 1935.

Not So Barmy Mick

Betty Lightfoot

Barmy Mick's talent knew no bounds
Silver-plated teapots: 'Offer me a pound!'
Teasets, Toy cars, whatever your needs —
(So long as your hand went up with speed)
His 'SPECIAL OFFER' starter went for a song:
'Half a crown now for this model of King Kong'

Barmy Mick's brainwave of selling his stock
In Auctioneer style meant he soon sold the lot!
Some days he'd offer his stall for fifty pound —
(This guaranteed him a cheer from the crowd)
His 'MONEYBACK OFFER' was the best around:
'Except on beakers you've bounced on the ground!'

Barmy Mick's cheek was never in doubt
He'd chew you up smartly, then spit you out
If you dared suggest his goods were at fault,
(He really was an expert at rubbing in salt)
His bargains were good, his prices were low:
'Who can I tempt to part with their dough?'

Barmy Mick's spiel as he swooped goods from stock
Was to hint that competitors' goods were 'HOT!'
His 'BARGAIN CORNER' was just the job,
(Ideal for Christmas presents costing ten bob)
But Barmy Mick's banter is heard no more —
Cross Lane Market's been tarmacked over.

The Salford Schoolboys' Strike of 1911

Ted Gray

Schoolchildren on strike! Unheard of – it couldn't happen! But it did – in Salford, in 1911!

What would prompt schoolboys to go on strike? Too much homework? Too short holidays? Too harsh discipline? In 1911 it may have been the power of example, for it was a sequel to a period of labour troubles in the district.

In July 1911, during the seamen's strike, dockers had struck in sympathy, and carters carrying goods to the docks had been attacked and their loads tipped into the roadway. Several mass meetings had taken place, missiles had been thrown at the police, and because of continuing riotous conduct, the Mayor of Salford had requested help from the Metropolitan Police. (The 250 members of that force accommodated in Cross Lane Barracks presented a silver cup on their departure, in gratitude to their hosts. This was used as the award for the annual rifle-shooting competition on the miniature range.) The Mayor also called in military help to preserve order. The carters joined the strike, and pickets prevented the movement of goods to and from the docks. In August, there was a strike of railway workers and Ship Canal employees, more mass meetings, plus general unrest amongst miners, all of which was followed in early September by a strike of workers at the Broughton Copper Works, and another at the flax mills, during which tramway men had been intimidated in an attempt to persuade them to stop work.

Consequently, the behaviour and tactics of the adult strikers would have been well-known to the children of the area, and it seems likely that as soon as the labour disputes had been settled, some of the older boys decided to copy what they had seen. The girls remained dignified and aloof from the proceedings, and only boys appear to have been involved.

The demands of the schoolboy strikers were:
1. All punishment should be abolished.
2. Boys should be allowed to leave school at 13 years of age.
3. Classroom monitors should receive twopence per week.
4. Every Wednesday afternoon should be a holiday.

Some of the bolder spirits also wanted a reduction of half-an-hour in both morning and afternoon school sessions, whilst others, realising the potential consequences of their actions, demanded that no one should be punished for going on strike. These demands were not formally submitted to the school authorities, but emerged from a series of disorganised rallies, usually held outside school gates.

The trouble started at Blackfriars Road on Monday lunchtime, the 11th September 1911, when a crowd of boys assembled outside the Council School and announced that they did not intend to return to their classrooms that afternoon. Having agreed that point, the boys then tried to persuade pupils at other schools to do the same. A group of about a dozen older boys organised a procession, which broke up when a police constable appeared on the horizon. Undeterred by this reverse, the ringleaders made their way to St. Simon's School, where they succeeded in persuading one more rebel to join their ranks, and then to St.Stephen's and Gravel Lane, where afternoon school had already commenced and where the potential recruits were out of their reach. Thus frustrated, the rebels put pleasure before business and went to the swimming baths.

At four o'clock they returned to Blackfriars Road School to intercept other boys coming out. They succeeded in extracting promises from many fellow-pupils not to return to school the following morning. However, during the evening a rumour spread rapidly around the district that the teachers were to be allowed a free hand in settling the strike, and that their choice of weapon was to be the birch ! In face of this prospect, courage seems to have evaporated, and the Blackfriars Road teachers were gratified to see an unusually full attendance on the Tuesday morning.

Elsewhere, however, the affair had been revitalised. Different rumours had spread overnight to other parts of the city, and it was reported that strikers were being encouraged by youths who had left school, and also by some mothers who wanted their children to be allowed to leave school to go to work at the age of thirteen. On that Tuesday morning a number of boys were reported absent from Marlborough Road School, but the main unrest centred on Regent Road, where the streets were thrown into chaos by hundreds of scholars parading around the district, holding 'meetings,' and trying to bring out pupils from schools not already affected. On the door of Regent Road School someone had chalked, "This school will be closed until further notice." The sign on Regent Road Bridge was even more startling: "This bridge will be blown up at one o'clock today." In another place appeared the legend: "We want us rites."

During the lunch hour 'pickets' wearing large home-made 'official badges' were stationed outside St.Joseph's School in West Craven Street, and at St.Clement's School in West Park Street, intercepting younger children and turning them away from school. Mothers then scattered the pickets, and escorted their children into the buildings.

The strikers, however, met with success in persuading the older pupils from St.Luke's School, Eccles New Road, to join them, and the combined force then marched to Seedley Council School on Liverpool Street. Here, they met with resistance from a policeman, who dispersed the procession by charging at the ranks all on his own. Other strikers had caused trouble at Hankinson Street School, where a firework had provided what the press referred to as a "sensational beginning," after which "the whole school was ripe for rebellion." A 'general strike' was called, but when the bell sounded for the start of afternoon school, all but about 70 pupils attended normally. The truants marched on John Street School, where they gained more sympathisers, and then to St.James' where everyone had gone into lessons. At Langworthy Road School the strikers expressed their disgust at the atmosphere of quiet, academic calm which pervaded the building, and made their way to Holland Croft for a 'meeting.' The 'meeting,' reported the local press, was notable for its "noise and feeble and disconnected oratory." In the midst of the proceedings, the young agitators espied a posse of three police constables approaching, and quickly dispersed.

Meanwhile, everything was proceeding very quietly in the schools, especially in those where boys were missing. One schoolmaster told a journalist from the 'Salford Reporter' that never before had he had to deal with such meek and well-behaved scholars. The truants were enjoying themselves, too. They rushed about from school to school, spreading the news that an important rally and 'demonstration' was to be convened on Holland's Croft at 8.30pm that night.

As it was raining that evening, nobody turned up for the big rally and demonstration, save for a lone journalist, who got wet whilst he was waiting for something to happen. The rebellion ended on the following morning with the unconditional surrender of the strikers. The majority of parents had not shown the slightest sympathy with the rebels, and the authorities had not paid any attention to their demands. The millennium which had been hoped for had not arrived, and the boys returned to school on the Wednesday morning in a chastened mood and with an uneasy feeling that the cane, which they had wanted to abolish, was likely to be in greater evidence than before.

[N.B. Contrary to malicious rumour, the writer of this article did not take part in the schoolboys' strike. He gained his information from the several press reports of September 1911.]

Troops were deployed in Salford during the 1911 dock strike, when it is thought that the example set by adults prompted the schoolboy strike described in the article. Mounted soldiers are seen here on Broad Street.

A 'Snappy Tapper'

Marjorie Frankland

Most little girls must dream, as I did, of appearing on the stage. I was lucky, however, for I achieved my ambition at a very early age. I was only four years old when my mother took me to Tootal Drive to join Ethel Holland's "Snappy Tappers."

There were several dancing schools in Salford at this time (1948), but Ethel Holland's had the reputation of being one of the best. How we all managed to fit into that small house on Tootal Drive I cannot now imagine. We hung our coats on a row of pegs in the kitchen, changed into our tap shoes, and then went into the back room where we had our lessons. This room had in it only a piano and a tap mat. It was a very superior mat, made up of fine wood struts which rolled up, not at all like my own home-made one, which we kept in our cellar and brought upstairs to practice on. I attended twice each week, one individual lesson after school, and a group lesson on Saturdays. Travelling from Weaste along Tootal Drive was a special treat for me, for we rode on the single-deck bus on route number 5, which seemed at the time more fun than riding on the normal double-deckers on numbers 1 and 3 services, which my family used to journey to Pendleton Church or Cross Lane market.

On Saturdays we prepared for our many concerts and examinations. Most of our concerts took place in the evenings in church halls all around the city. One of my favourite venues was the 'Little Mission' at the bottom of Derby Road. Each of us had our own spot on the programme, and at the end of each half we all came together in one large spectacular number. At the concerts we were accompanied on the piano by a gentleman we knew only as 'Uncle Arthur.' He always played slightly faster than Ethel Holland, who played for rehearsals, and we had to speed-up our dancing to keep up with him. Many costumes were required, and much ingenuity went into the making of them, particularly when I first joined, for it was just after the end of the war, when material was still hard to come by. My mother must have spent hours cutting cloth, sewing on sequins, making hats, etc. There were occasions when even my father was enlisted to help. Being a cabinet-maker, he was able to construct several props for me, including the tap mat.

My very first dance routine was to the tune "Ballin' The Jack," after which I progressed to "Polly Wolly Doodle," and then to a dance in partnership with another couple, a brother and sister, to a tune called "Dearie." This was a very popular number, which earned us a good deal of praise at concerts. We always played to full houses, as our kind of entertainment was very popular. It was very exciting being 'made up' by our mothers before each performance. I had a full range of theatrical make-up, which we bought from a shop in Manchester. The make-up had to be applied in a special way, and we had to learn the technique as part of our 'theory' classes when taking examinations for medals awarded by the 'S.A.T.D.' (the Supreme Association of Teachers and Dancers). Some of our examinations were held at the Beechwood Studios, a well-known dance academy on Eccles

Old Road, managed by Ena Adams, but we also had to venture as far afield as Rochdale Road, Harpurhey, to the dance studios of Gladys Peach.

One of the highlights of my dancing career came in 1951, when the nation celebrated the Festival of Britain. Our contribution was a collection of dances all related to King and Country. I danced a number called "Soldiers Of The King."

I well remember some of the dancers who were older than me. I hoped one day to dance as well as they did, and in particular I admired the musical comedy number "We're A Couple Of Swells," and a dance by one of the boys, "Anchors Aweigh." My all-time favourite was "Me And My Shadow," danced by two girls, one small and dressed in a white tail coat, the other taller and dressed identically in black.

I carried on with my dancing lessons until I was about eleven, and then changed to ballroom dancing. I have many happy memories of my dancing years, and even now, when I hear any of the old tunes to which I performed, I can imagine I am on stage again at the 'Little Mission.'

The Salford 'Snappy Tappers' Dance Troupe in 1949, Marjorie Frankland in front row, extreme left, with teacher Ethel Frost (nee Holland) centre.

The War Years in the Dock Office, Manchester Ship Canal, 1939-1945

M. G. Ingham

Immediately behind the imposing Trafford Road entrance gates to the Docks lay the Dock Offices, a relatively modern building, opened in 1927. Inside, the imposing entrance foyer with marbled floor was supervised by a uniformed Commissionaire. A wide stairway and lift led to the upper floors. In the period of the Second World War, in order to make it less conspicuous from the air, the rendered elevations and roof of the building were covered with a mosaic of camouflage paint.

There were very few private offices in the building, the majority of the clerical staff being accommodated in large open areas, containing possibly 200 clerks. The first thing one noticed on entering any of the main departments was the incredible level of noise from the numerous voices. The furniture consisted of high stools and double-sided polished timber desks, some as long as 15 feet, with twin brass rails fitted over the centre, on which the ledgers were kept. Pedestal-type telephones, with the ear-piece on a flex, were provided on most desks, but there was little else in the way of equipment. One large electrically-operated calculator was available, provided the user was able to decimalize the pounds, shillings, and pence, and then re-convert the answer.

There was a 'typing pool' of about 50 ladies, all housed in one location under the eagle eye and imposing presence of Miss Long. Other than private secretaries, who worked in the smaller offices of the managers, the pool typists carried out the typing and copying of all the correspondence of the main offices. Because men aged between 18 and 45 had been 'called up' for war service, the work force in the building seemed to comprise mainly the young and old of both sexes.

Lunch (then called dinner) could be taken at the Staff Canteen, opposite the Dock Office, until this building was destroyed in a air raid. The canteen was then housed in part of a warehouse at the side of No.8 Dock. The sights and smells of the contents of dock warehouses were of considerable variety. The most obnoxious odour came from wet salted hides, imported from South America. An alternative eating place was the 'British Restaurant' on Trafford Road, which provided a hot meal, with pudding, for something like one shilling and sixpence. The steamed jam roll and custard is well-remembered.

During the war, the Docks operated at full stretch, with ships, cranes, lorries, and internal railways providing perpetual movement 24 hours per day. Male staff were required to remain on the premises overnight once per fortnight for fire-watch duties. Brief training in fire-fighting, first aid, and emergency procedures in the event of a gas attack, had been given to all taking part in this night duty roster. However, most nights passed uneventfully once the main attack was over, and the rest of the time was spent at a snooker table, or playing cards or darts. On duty nights, tea and breakfast were provided at the canteen.

There were visits from former members of staff, who invariably called in when on leave from the Armed Forces, though, sadly, a number of them were never to return.

Most people were required to work on Saturday mornings. A holiday list was passed round, first choice going to senior staff, no duplication being allowed. Junior staff were lucky to get a week in March or October.

Office discipline was maintained at all times, everyone 'clocking' in or out. A queue of staff with hats and coats formed at the clock as the main leaving times approached, waiting for the clock to show the passing of the appropriate minute. Anyone who 'clocked off' early could expect to be admonished. Then followed the rush to catch trams or buses, or pedal away on cycles.

The most memorable part of the war years at the Docks was undoubtedly in witnessing the after-effects of the 1940 blitz. The demolished buildings, the unexploded land mines, the fires, and the sunken ship in No.9 Dock remain vivid in the mind's eye. But, apart from these sad recollections, I have good memories of friendships - and I did meet my wife there!

The Dock Office, pictured here in 1935, was new in 1927.

"Watchin' t' Scholars"

_____ *Roy Bullock*

Although they are still going on, if only in a small way, the annual Whit Walks revive memories of the grand affairs of long ago. Preparations for the great day started weeks in advance, with mothers and friends busy with sewing machines and needle-and-thread, making up colour co-ordinated dresses of satin, taffeta, and lace for the girls. Some were designed from cheaply-bought remnants, others the result of weeks of saving from hard-pressed purses. The shilling-a-week 'clothing clubs' would often be used for savings to buy shoes, or other garments. I remember my two sisters having hand-crocheted dresses in white-and-green silk-type thread, certainly a one-off design which would probably cost hundreds of pounds at today's prices, if only because of the many hours spent in their making.

Come Whit Weekend, new clothes would be donned, and we children would be taken or sent round to our local relations to show-off our finery. Cries of, "Oooh, come in. Let's have a look at you. Don't you look nice?" Girls would twirl their dresses, whilst the boys would be thinking "Hurry up. Let's get it over with. I want to play out." Grannies and other elderly relations always seemed to want to go the whole hog, and do a full body search. "Let's have a look at your underwear. Oooh, isn't that nice?" Presumably, this was an excuse to check that everything was new. But then came the big moment. "Now, where's my purse?" Eventually, a threepenny bit, or a 'tanner,' or, if you were very lucky, a shilling would be pocketed, and off we went to visit as many others as could be fitted in. The same routine would ensue at each call, and, at last, we returned home, with pockets jingling, to change into normal, comfortable 'playing-out' clothes, with the enticing prospect of a quick dash to the toffee shop. Alas, sometimes the only dash was that of dashed hopes, when Mum said, "Here, where do you think you're off to? Hand it over. That's not for you. It's towards paying for your new clothes." Cries of "Oh, Mum," would fall unheeded, and eventually we might finish up with just a few pence for toffee or fruit.

In Whit Week, the 'Walks' for the Protestant churches were held on the Monday, those for the Catholics on the Friday. An early start was essential. First, there was a wash-down in the big brown kitchen sink (slopstone) or the tin bath brought in from the yard, then it was off to St.Philip's Church for about 8.30 a.m. It was an early start for fathers, too, because the public houses along Chapel Street used to open early (and illegally). Perhaps the police turned a blind eye on these occasions.

The processions would form up and make their way into Manchester via Chapel Street. The long columns of marchers from Ordsall, Pendleton, Whit Lane, Broughton, etc. would converge and move into Albert Square, where they met other churches and schools from all parts of Manchester. Reputedly, there were often up to 30,000 marchers taking part in a celebration, which, to date, has lasted 191 years. After a service in Albert Square, the processions would prepare for the return journey. In my time, the Salford churches would return to Chapel Street via Deansgate. By that time, usually round about noon, the streets would be thronged with thousands of people, standing six deep on the pavements in places, hanging out of upstairs windows, even climbing up lamp posts - anywhere to gain a better view. The dads, of course, would be propping-up the pub window sills. The marchers would pass by in a seemingly never-ending procession, interspersed with pipe bands, brass bands, silver bands, boy scouts and cubs, girl guides and brownies, members of mothers' unions, church wardens, mounted police,

mothers pushing prams, people in wheel-chairs - everyone wanting to be part of the occasion. Splashes of bright colours would be added by the young girls in colour co-ordinated dresses. They were often carrying little banners, declaring them to be "God's Little Garden," or "God's Little Rainbow."

There would be assorted cries and instructions from the onlookers. "Hold your lily up." "Pick your feet up !" "Stop gawping." "You're out of step." And, of course, the inevitable "You hoo," to attract the attention of a walker to a friend in the

Typical of the many Whit Walkers is this group of children from St.John's Church, Irlams O'Th'Height, seen in Bolton Road in the 1950s.

crowd. Some years, if it rained on the walkers of one faith, but the sun shone on the others, there would be the good-humoured observations of "God knows his own." There were always cheers when the flamboyant drum majors tossed their batons high into the air, and even greater cheers if they failed to catch them on their descent. There always seemed to be a very big man playing the bass drum, and similar individuals seemed to be selected to carry the large banners, which must have been very difficult to control on windy days.

The bands had a somewhat repetitive repertoire of tunes. 'The Happy Wanderer' seemed to be the popular favourite in my day. The crowds always seemed very patriotic, with red-and-blue 'shakers' and a sprinkling of miniature union jacks to wave as the processions passed. Some watchers wore union jack clothes and hats, and some of the tunes selected had a martial flavour, like 'Sons Of The Sea,' 'Boys Of The Bulldog Breed,' and 'Bless 'Em All.' Perhaps this was because it was wartime.

Eventually, the last of the marchers passed, and then the crowds slowly dispersed, the dads still leaning on the pub window sills, seemingly reluctant to depart. Mothers would follow the walkers, ready to collect their children when the procession reached base. Afterwards, all the public houses would be full, and there would be music and a sing-song in every one. Sandwiches and pickles were provided, and a good time was had by all. Fathers would reappear from the town centre pubs, and some would give a song. At closing time, children would hang around outside, hoping their cries of "Any spare change, mister?" would fall on easy prey. Some men would scatter a handful of coins in the air in order to enjoy the sight of the mad scramble which followed. Occasionally, accordions or 'squeeze boxes' which had been played in the pubs, would be played all the way home, to the delight of cheering children.

The Whit Walks were glories which will probably never be achieved again. This year, about 5000 walkers paraded in Manchester, and a small contingent came along Chapel Street, but the watching crowds have gone. The churches of St.George's Charlestown, St.Cyprian's, St.James' Hope, and St.Philip's still 'carried the banner,' so to speak, this year finishing at St.Philip's. Only in Albert Square and around Market Street did the crowds of spectators reach any size. Surprisingly, many people are not aware that the Whit Walks still take place, probably because the days are no longer designated 'Whit Monday' or 'Whit Friday,' but, more usually, the 'May Bank Holiday.' It is a shame that an event which gave so much happiness, entertainment, and pride, has now declined.

Incidentally, whilst 'watching the scholars' in Manchester this year, 1992, I witnessed something which hadn't happened for over 40 years. The procession held up a tram!

When every Penny Counted, 1930–1945

Eric Proctor

In the 1930s the effects of the Depression made life difficult for many families. Luckily, my father had a job with the Highways Department, and later with Salford Transport, earning about 30 shillings per week. Priorities were strictly enforced by my mother. First, pay the rent. Next, feed the family. Create the best home possible. Never, never go into debt. With three youngsters to feed and clothe, every penny was allocated carefully.

Langworthy Road School

When I started school in the mid-1930s, the Headteacher of the Langworthy Road Infant School was Miss Holmes. I recall her giving out hot 'Horlicks' for our winter playtime drink. My first class photograph was taken by the ubiquitous Stansfeld Parker, whose prints recorded my progress through Elementary and then Grammar School. Years later, when I became a teacher, you can guess who was hiding behind the black-clothed tripod to record my class - yes, Stansfeld Parker again. He must have photographed most Salford schools and pupils over the years.

The traditional garb for many children was a knitted jersey and tie. Sometimes, this covered a 'liberty bodice !' The play area for mixed infants joined on to the older girls' yard, and trespassing brought trouble. Next came the "big boys' yard," where mixing was prevented by railings. Thus, at the age of seven, boys and girls separated, and my peers were always male only until I went to a mixed Teacher-Training College.

We moved into the "Big Boys'" — on the top floor — with some foreboding. Headmaster Mr.Dirkin had a reputation for strictness, punctuality, and excessive length of cane, closely rivalled, it was rumoured, by some of his staff. But I adored my first teacher in that department. 'Maggie' Robertson walked daily from her home in Oakfield Terrace, near Peel Park, and if we passed in the street, we raised a cap. If capless, we saluted. She was a typical spinster schoolma'am, but she could teach. One of her strengths was teaching by rote, and I still recall with accuracy the 'money table,' the 'Good Samaritan,' etc. In her class I had my first textbook with coloured pictures, a Geography book about an African boy. Try as I would, I rarely came to terms with pen and ink. Clods of blotting paper ended up in the ink-well, and I always managed to get more ink on my hands than in the book. Many activities were carried on in a military fashion — lining-up in the playground ; giving-out materials ; entering and leaving class ; and physical education (called 'Drill').

Amongst the teachers I encountered were Mr.Dickenson, Mr.Hancock, Mr.Halpern, Mr.Oldham, and Mr.Wansell (who later became the Headteacher). Several of the male teachers were later called-up for war service. There was also Mr.Salter, who played the piano. From Mr.Salter's class I passed the scholarship examination after sitting a test at Halton Bank School. (Little did I imagine then that 24 years later I would succeed him as Headteacher of Regent Road School.) 'Passing the scholarship' was a great credit to the school, but, in fact, very few from Langworthy Road sat the test, as many parents had limited aspirations for their children. The school-leaving age was then 14, and many saw the gaining of apprenticeships or other jobs as an urgent priority in augmenting the family income. Going on to the Grammar School meant staying as a student until at least the age of 16, an obligation many parents did not wish to undertake, particularly as the war had started.

I remember well the visits of a Police Sergeant, of ample proportions, who taught us to sing the road safety song:

"When you cross the road, by day or night,
Remember the dangers that loom in sight,
Look to the left, and look to the right,
And you'll never, never get run over."

Then there were the days when we had to place our frozen milk bottles in front of the open fire in the classroom to melt the ice ; going by tramcar from Eccles New Road to school sports at Belle Vue ; seeing the daily trek of child refugees from the Spanish Civil War who used the Quaker Church on Langworthy Road (now the Royal British Legion

Langworthy Road, Seedley, centre of the writer's boyhood activities. The buildings have not changed a great deal, though the shops on the left have lost their verandahs.

Club) as their school; being very late after watching a lame horse, which had to be shot, on the corner of Seedley Road; and envying the Standard 7 boys who went down into the cellar for Woodwork classes, whilst the older girls went up to Halton Bank for 'Laundry Lessons.'

Shopping Mecca

Shopping for perishables such as bread, butter, meat. or fish, was a daily chore. Our only cold store was a slab of stone in the scullery, so purchases were often consumed on the same day. Summertime in food stores was accompanied by the unpleasant sight of flies and blue-bottles trapped on sticky fly-papers, which were unrolled and hung from the ceilings. Rabbits suspended by the dozen were common, but chicken was a rare luxury, usually seen only at Christmas time. Most food was weighed out by the shop assistants, with just a few pre-packed items.

Langworthy Road was an excellent shopping centre, and the Co-Op alone had five large departments: Butchery, Grocery, Gents' Outfitting, Ladies' Wear, and Shoes. My mother regarded shopping at the Co-Op as a way of saving, for the receipt checks, which were stuck on to gummed sheets, qualified at quarter end for 'divi,' which enabled us to buy items not allowed for in the weekly budget, such as shoes and clothes. On Saturday afternoons, an office was opened above the shops for the Co-Op's 'Penny Bank.'

Money To Spend

In 1938 or 1939 my parents had saved enough to take the family on holiday to Blackpool for a week. The first part of each day was spent shopping for food, which was taken back for the boarding house owner to cook. The other holiday which I remember was a Sunday School outing to Southport - for a day!

About this time, I made my first contribution to the family budget. I was taken on as a 'helper' to the Co-Op milkman. I used to dash from school at 12 noon and help until 1.00 p.m., but at weekends I was able to join him from 7.30am until 2.00pm. We pushed a 'dandy,' a large-wheeled wooden cart, purpose-built for holding the chained churns, from which we ladled the milk. Householders would leave empty jugs, together with the necessary money or tokens (bought at the Co-Op grocery store), on doorsteps or window-sills, with a net or saucer to cover the top of the jug when filled. It was not unusual for the front door to be left unlocked so that we could walk in to deliver the milk. How proud I was to take home my 'wages,' only a few pence, of which I was allowed to keep half. Gradually, bottled milk became the norm, with cardboard milk tops, opened by pressing-through a centre circle - very useful for play and modelling.

We also liked to 'help' the night watchman. Road works always seemed to be accompanied by a workmen's hut and a coke-fired brazier, and from 5.00pm or 6.00pm the watchman mounted guard until the next morning. The company of youngsters must have been a welcome relief before the long, lonely hours of darkness. His 'helpers' would vie to re-stack the coke, or whatever, until called in for bed.

Anticipated joy was realised at weekend. Pay day was Friday, and also time to collect the 'Saturday penny,' which would buy two ounces of sweets. More often than not, the choice would fall upon spearmint bars, liquorice, or chocolate cigarettes. Other favourites included 'Football Mixtures' (striped boiled sweets), Chocolate Chewing Nuts, and Whipped Cream Walnuts. Potato crisps were 'plain,' but the bags included the little blue salt packet.

I found three other sources of income. First, came a short spell helping at Screeton's wood yard on Jessel Street, close to the Royal Hotel (now the 'Flat Iron'). Mr. Jessel had a horse-drawn cart, on which he toured the neighbourhood selling bundles of firewood. In the yard, an open and unguarded circular saw, cut the wood into lengths. I chopped these lengths into small pieces known as 'faggots,' which were then put in a vice to be gripped by a piece of stout wire. I was promoted to the bundling job, but was sometimes unable to fasten the wire tightly enough. When my pay was docked because the bundles were loose, a letter from my mother, containing vague threats as to what might ensue if I was not paid, brought prompt results in the way of payment, but also ensured the termination of my employment. I always regretted not having had the chance to go round the streets on the cart.

My next career came in the 1940s, when I ran a 'football sweep.' It was probably quite illegal, but many neighbours joined in this, a not uncommon venture. Fifty numbered tickets were picked out of a tin by clients at twopence per try. The winner was determined by the combined scores in Salford's rugby match, or, when Salford ceased playing during the war, by Dewsbury's game. I paid out five shillings as the prize, and my reward was the excess - up to three shillings and fourpence if I sold all the tickets, which was rare. My customers were very loyal, thrilled when they won, and always curious to know, "Who won last week?"

The third source of income appeared when I was 12 years old and able to act as a newspaper delivery boy on a round which covered part of Langworthy Road, Castleway, and Bolton Road as far as Chaseley. I gained permission from the caretaker at Pendleton High School for Girls to take a short cut through the grounds from the gate on Chaseley Road. It saved me a great distance, and the caretaker gained an earlier delivery at his house on Eccles Old Road, which was my last call. One day, at about 5.30 p.m., I took my short cut as usual, only to be confronted by a dignified Miss Whale, the Headmistress, demanding to know what a *boy* was doing in her school grounds. She accepted my explanation, but

with ill grace. Afterwards, I felt guilty, for I must have been the only boy permitted to enter the hallowed grounds.

Play At Little Cost
In the 1930s children's games did not depend upon manufactured items bought from a shop. A tightly-rolled and tied bundle of newspapers or rags, even a stone, substituted for a football. But if we used a tin can to kick about, we were reprimanded – local superstition held that the rattle was a 'sign of death.' (Cynics claimed that this particular superstition was probably started by a mother who wanted a quiet afternoon, the 'death' being that of the child making the noise!) Possession of a metal hoop, or an old tyre to roll along the pavements, was heaven. The game of 'piggy' needed nothing more than a small piece of wood, whittled at both ends, and a stick to strike it with as it bounced up from a hard rap on one end. The almost traffic-free streets were ours for games: tag; hide and seek; ralevo; Cowboys and Indians; whip and top, with a home-made whip; marbles; football; and cricket. Seedley and Buile Hill parks nearby were safe, with swings and a duck-pond, where we would try our luck at catching tiddlers. Woe betide you if you were seen climbing the railings, and one of the park-keepers was within chasing distance! The bowling greens were sacred. The Museum, with the stuffed elephant on the top floor, and the three (cold, warm, and hot) inter-connected green-houses, were big attractions. The Seedley Park entrance path, with flower beds on both sides right up to the bowling green, was a visual delight.

On dark nights, the lamp-lighter turned on the street gas lamps, and in the pools of light, or outside the lighted shop windows, we would gather to chat and play. Many houses had cellar grids, down which deliveries of coal were tipped, and it was thought to be a great joke to tie together the door knocker and the grid – wise folk would fit an internal chain to the grid to forestall this kind of prank.

A visit to the cinema was a treat, and there were no qualms about asking an adult, "Will you take me in, please?" if the film happened to be classified. At home, we possessed a wind-up clockwork gramophone, with a limited stock of 78 rpm records. We boys were allowed to use it under supervision, but we must have spent nearly as much time winding it up and changing the needles, as listening to the music. Our records included, "In A Monastery Garden," "Motoring Without Tears" (a music-hall sketch about learning to drive a car), and a monologue by 'Stainless Stephen,' a radio comedian, who, on our record, extolled the virtues of tripe.

Children's comics were usually obtained second-hand, or by swapping for some other possession. We loved the 'Dandy,' 'Beano,' 'Wizard,' 'Adventure,' 'Hotspur,' and so on. Clockwork toys were precious, and appeared only on birthdays or at Christmas. Few women smoked, so for boys a "Smoker's Outfit" was a great present - all the items were made of chocolate, and we could pretend to puff away in imitation of our male elders. Spinning tops, roller skates, marbles, and yo-yos would appear according to those 'seasons' which used to begin and end so mysteriously. The comic 'Annuals' were read over and over again throughout the year.

Illness

The cost of medical care was a constant burden. The long-established Langworthy Road doctors (Elias, McKinty, and Parker) had their own pharmacist, who made up medicines at the surgery, but also doubled up as "The Doctors' Man," calling round weekly to collect sixpence to pay off the account. Successors in the practice, Dr. Gould and Dr. Gibb, continued into the 1980s. Mr. C.R.V. Haynes, the local dentist, was a dignified and respected gentleman, who for many years served on the Salford Council and eventually became Mayor. His daughter Rosemary was the anaesthetist,. She had a lovely soothing voice for singing to you as you lost consciousness! In the late 1930s the Haynes bachelor sons owned a sports car, so we thought of them as being very rich. Even at that date, many goods were still delivered by horse-drawn vehicles, such as those used by Royle's bakery. Piles of horse-droppings on the cobbled streets were commonplace, and gardeners would collect them by the bucketful for use on their allotments.

Resilience Needed

Life in the home was physically demanding. All our hot water had to be carried from fire to scullery in a large heavy kettle. Clothes were washed by hand, then ironed using a block heated on the fire. Life had as many rituals as religion. Customs included donkey-stoning the steps and pavement outside the house on Friday afternoons, black-leading the grate and fire-irons, the weekly bath-night, and the annual lime-washing of the cellar and outside toilet.

My brothers and I attended St. Ambrose's Sunday School, and for the annual Whit Walks, a new suit, usually made for us by a lady in the next street, was essential.

My father moved to regular night work, and the extra pay enabled us to have electricity installed in 1936. Then the family could cluster round the radio to hear stars of the music hall, etc., and I remember well listening to the commentary when cricketer Len Hutton broke the run record. We considered ourselves somewhat superior to those unfortunates who had only a battery set, and who had to take a weekly trip to the local radio shop to have the accumulators charged.

Within the neighbourhood, those who depended upon the pawnshop were well-known. One particular lady wheeled a pram to Ridgeway's shop, in Church Street, at 9.00 a.m. every Monday morning. The pram was said to contain her husband's suit, which had been worn for the weekend's jollity, and which would remain in the pawnshop until the next pay-day.

World War 2

The outbreak of war in 1939 shattered our normal lives. Within a few weeks we had sand-bags blocking-up the cellar windows, black-out material had been fitted to all other windows, and gas masks had been issued from Langworthy Road School. People with only a back-yard tried to grow vegetables to help the war effort. School dinners became common. An anti-aircraft barrage balloon appeared in Buile Hill Park. Our back-entries were concreted-over in sections for outdoor air raid shelters, and indoors we had a large metal cage, which doubled as a table during the day, and a family bedroom at night when the raids came. The sounding of sirens after 10.00 p.m., meant that we could arrive at school at 10.00am the next day. To conserve imported fuel, a few of Salford's buses were converted to run on gas, produced in trailers towed behind - they were not very powerful, and struggled to climb Langworthy Road hill. Often in the evenings, we made peg rugs. Without thought of danger, we melted lead in a tin on the open fire, and poured it into plaster moulds to make our own model soldiers, submarines, or aircraft. Such was the influence of international affairs on our little world, that we even made 'non-aggression' pacts with rival gangs of children.

Possession of a battery torch was essential in the black-out, which lasted until the fear of air attacks diminished in 1945. Victory in Europe (V.E. Day, 8th May 1945) saw some memorable street parties, and celebrations continued, with houses and streets festooned with flags and bunting as servicemen returned home. More followed after victory over Japan (V.J. Day, 15th August 1945), and peace was restored at last.

Life since the war has been dominated by an ever-increasing rate of technological change and greater provision of creature comforts. I wonder whether many of us would be prepared to give up our central heating, micro-wave ovens, television sets, video-recorders, electronic calculators, and so on, if only we could enjoy again the trust, safety and orderliness of our yesteryears.

The Working Days of a Trolley-boy

Victor Aitchison

Gaining a job as a trolley-boy on the Salford Tramways was not easy. Before an applicant was granted an interview, he had to produce two written testimonials from persons of some standing in the community. Relatives were disbarred from providing any recommendations. My references were kindly supplied by Doctor Rifkin and Councillor Higginbottom, and I had to take them to be checked by a Supervisor, a Mr. Bell.

Then the applicant had to wait and see if he was going to be invited for an interview. When the day came, I had to answer all sorts of questions from Mr. Bell and the General Manager, Mr. Moffett, and then had to go home and wait again for the result. On being invited for a second interview, I was instructed to bring my mother with me. This was to make sure that I really wanted the job. My mother told them that if I did not become a trolley-boy, I would be very upset. I don't know whether this did any good, but I became a trolley-boy.

So, in 1929, at the age of 15, I went to collect my uniform. It had to be the right fit, because all trolley-boys were expected to look smart. Then, with the other new boys, I was given a week's training. Duties and safety measures were explained, and we were shown how to turn the trolley when a tramcar was ready to reverse, place the trolley-wheel on the overhead wire, change the points, and generally assist the adult members of the crew. It was emphasised that we had to be polite to passengers, and help them all we could, especially the elderly or infirm.

It was a proud day for me when I turned up for my first day's work. My mother made sure that my boots were always well-polished and that my trousers were always well pressed. Before work commenced, the boys were inspected by Mr. Bell, who checked that buttons were shiny, collars were clean, etc. He would sometimes say things like, "Tell your mother you want a hair cut." But, looking back, I think to myself that those were good days. My first wage packet contained eleven shilings and sixpence (about $57^1/_2$p in today's money), but it seemed a fortune then. I gave the packet unopened to my mother, and she gave me half-a-crown (25p) to spend. My father had been killed during the war in 1916, so my mother, like many women who had lost their husbands in 1914-18, had not had an easy time.

Eventually, I was promoted to be a points-boy, working at the busy junction of Deansgate and Blackfriars Street at St. Mary's Gate. Here, the trams could go in any direction, and it was my job to see that the points and the overhead wires were set correctly for whichever way the tramcar was bound. I also had to keep an eye on the policeman directing the traffic, so as to avoid any accident or misunderstanding. Busy, but happy, days!

The crew of a Salford tramcar pose for the photographer at the Swinton terminus. Driver and guard occupy a more important position on the step, whilst the trolley-boy stands in the roadway. Manchester and Salford were the only towns ever to employ the third member of crew, and the trolley-boys were expected to move up to the position of guard or driver as they grew older.

NORTHERN CLASSIC REPRINTS

The Manchester Man

(Mrs. G. Linnaeus Banks)

Re-printed from an 1896 illustrated edition — undoubtedly the finest limp-bound edition ever. Fascinating reading, includes Peterloo. Over 400 pages, wonderfully illustrated.

ISBN 1 872226 16 7   £4.95

The Manchester Rebels

(W Harrison Ainsworth)

A heady mixture of fact and fiction combined in a compelling story of the Jacobean fight for the throne of England. Manchester's involvement and the formation of the Manchester Regiment. Authentic illustrations.

ISBN 1 872226 29 9   £4.95

Hobson's Choice (the Novel)

(Harold Brighouse)

The humorous and classic moving story of Salford's favourite tale. Well worth re-discovering this enjoyable story. Illustrated edition. Not been available since 1917, never before in paperback.

ISBN 1 872226 36 1   £4.95

Stories and Tales Of Old Manchester

(Frank Hird, edited Cliff Hayes)

A ramble through Manchester's history, many lesser known stories brought to life, informative yet human book. Over 50 stories.

ISBN 1 872226 22 1   £4.95

Stories & Tales Of Old Lancashire

(Frank Hird)

Over 70 fascinating tales told in a wonderful light-hearted fashion. Witches, seiges and superstitions, battles and characters all here.

ISBN 1 872226 21 3   £4.95

Poems & Songs Of Lancashire

(Edwin Waugh)

A wonderful quality reprint of a classic book by undoubtedly one of Lancashire's finest poets. First published 1859 faithfully reproduced. Easy and pleasant reading, a piece of history.

ISBN 1 872226 27 2   £4.95

The Best of Old Lancashire — Poetry & Verse

Published in 1866 as the very best of contemporary Lancashire writing, this book now offers a wonderful insight into the cream of Lancashire literature in the middle of the last century. Nearly 150 years later, edited and republished, the book now presents a unique opportunity to read again the masters of our past.

ISBN 1 872226 50 7   £4.95

The Dock Road

(J. Francis Hall RN)

A seafaring tale of old Liverpool. Set in the 1860s, with the American Civil War raging and the cotton famine gripping Lancashire. Period illustrations.

ISBN 1 872226 37 X   £4.95

The Lancashire Witches

(W. Harrison Ainsworth)

A beautifully illustrated edition of the most famous romance of the supernatural.

ISBN 1 872226 55 8   £4.95

Stories Of Great Lancastrians

(written Frank Hird)

The lives of 24 great men of the county, told in easy reading style. Complete with sketches and drawings, a good introduction to the famous of Lancashire and Manchester. John Byrom, Arkwright, Tim Bobbins, Duke of Bridgewater.

ISBN 1 872226 23 X   £4.95

OTHER LOCAL PUBLICATIONS

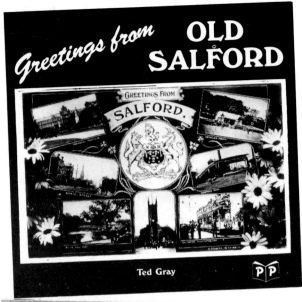

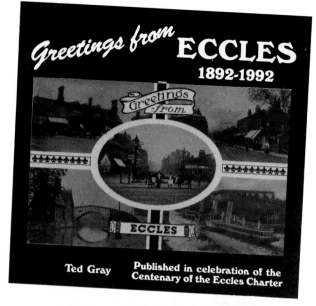

ALSO NORTH WALES, WIRRAL, LIVERPOOL, LANCASHIRE COAST, YORKSHIRE COAST AND THE HEART OF LANCASHIRE